food with flair

photography by Jean Cazals

SILVERBACK

First published in 2004 by
Quadrille Publishing Limited
Alhambra House
27-31 Charing Cross Road
London WC2H OLS

This edition published by Silverback Books, Inc.
San Francisco, California
www.silverbackbooks.com

ISBN 1-59637-008-4

Creative Director Helen Lewis
Editorial Director Jane O'Shea
Consultant Editor Janet Illsley
Photographic Direction Vanessa Courtier
Senior Designer Jim Smith
Editor Jane Keskeys
Production Beverley Richardson

Printed in China

Cookery notes
All recipes serve 4 unless otherwise stated. All spoon measures are level
unless otherwise indicated. Follow either metric or imperial measures, not
a mixture of both as they are not necessarily interchangeable. Use fresh
herbs and freshly ground black pepper unless otherwise suggested.

Contents

starters

Scallops with fava bean purée

12 large scallops, cleaned
3 tablespoons extra-virgin olive oil
salt and pepper
1 tablespoon lemon juice
For the fava bean purée
¾ cup fava beans
½ garlic clove, crushed

1 tablespoon freshly grated
  Parmesan cheese
1 tablespoon chopped fresh mint
2 tablespoons extra virgin olive oil
4 tablespoons heavy cream
For the garnish
mint sprigs

1 Cut away the tough muscle at the side of each scallop and any dark vein, then wash and dry well. Toss with 1 tablespoon of the oil, season liberally, and then set aside.

2 To make the fava bean purée, cook the beans in lightly salted boiling water for 3–4 minutes until tender. Drain well and transfer to a blender. Add the remaining ingredients, except the cream, and purée until smooth. Transfer to a small pan, add the cream, and warm through. Keep warm.

3 Heat a ridged grill or heavy-based pan until smoking, add the scallops, and cook for 1 minute, then turn and cook the other side for 1 minute. Transfer to a warm plate and rest for another 1 minute.

4 For the dressing, mix the remaining 2 tablespoons oil with the lemon juice and seasoning. Arrange the scallops on individual plates with the bean purée. Drizzle with the dressing and garnish with mint to serve.

Note The bean purée can be prepared ahead. To serve, add the cream and heat through.

A creamy minted bean purée is the perfect partner to sweet, chargrilled scallops.

Indian spiced monkfish chappatis

2 monkfish fillets, each ½ pound, skinned
1 garlic clove, crushed
1 teaspoon grated fresh gingerroot
1 tablespoon tandoori spice mix
1 tablespoon tomato purée
1 tablespoon sunflower oil
1½ tablespoon lemon juice
For the raita
⅜ cup yogurt
¼ teaspoon salt

¼ teaspoon sugar
pinch of cayenne pepper
generous 1-inch chunk cucumber, peeled and grated
1 tablespoon chopped fresh mint
To finish
2 chappatis, cut into triangles
sunflower oil, for shallow frying
lemon wedges and mint leaves, to garnish

1 Place the fillets in a dish. In a small bowl, mix together the garlic, ginger, tandoori spice, tomato purée, oil, and lemon juice. Add to the fish, turn to coat, and then leave to marinate in a cool place for at least 1 hour.
2 Meanwhile, mix together the ingredients for the raita. Set aside.
3 Preheat the broiler. Lay the fish on the broiler rack and broil for 6–8 minutes, turning halfway, until cooked through. Leave to rest in a warm place for 5 minutes.
4 Meanwhile, heat a thin layer of oil in a skillet and fry the chappati triangles for 1 minute until crisp. Drain on paper towels.
5 Slice the fish and sandwich between the chappati triangles. Serve garnished with lemon and mint, accompanied by the raita.

Broiled monkfish fillets infused with tandoori spices are served between crisp fried chappatis, with a cooling cucumber raita.

Shrimp wonton soup

5 cups vegetable stock

4 red chiles, bruised

2 slices fresh gingerroot

2 tablespoons rice vinegar

2 tablespoons light soy sauce

2 teaspoons sugar

1 teaspoon sesame oil

For the wontons

6 ounces small raw shrimp, peeled

4 ounces fresh cod fillet, skinned
   and diced

2 green onions, chopped

1 garlic clove, crushed

grated rind and juice of ½ lime

1 tablespoons chopped fresh cilantro
   leaves

salt and pepper

20 wonton wrappers

1 small egg, beaten

For the garnish

cilantro sprigs

1 Put the stock into a pan with the chiles, ginger, rice vinegar, soy sauce, sugar, and sesame oil. Bring to the boil, cover, and simmer gently for about 20 minutes.

2 Devein the shrimp, wash, and pat dry. Put in a food processor with the cod, green onions, garlic, lime rind, and juice, and the cilantro. Purée until fairly smooth, then season with a little salt and pepper.

3 Brush each wonton wrapper with a little beaten egg and place a spoonful of the shrimp mixture in the center. Draw the edges up over the filling, and pinch together at the top to form small parcels.

4 Drop the wontons into the soup, return to a rolling boil, and then simmer for 3–4 minutes.

5 Ladle the soup into warmed bowls. Serve garnished with cilantro sprigs.

You can buy the wonton wrappers for this fragrant soup from oriental food stores.

Garlic shrimp and mozzarella salad

20 large raw shrimp, peeled
3 tablespoons extra virgin olive oil
2 garlic cloves, crushed
1 red chilli, seeded and chopped
8 ounces buffalo mozzarella cheese, sliced
4 ripe plum tomatoes, sliced

For the basil oil
handful fresh basil leaves
4 tablespoons extra-virgin olive oil
½ teaspoon lemon juice
salt and pepper
For the garnish
basil leaves

1 Start by making the basil oil. Roughly tear the leaves and place in a blender with the oil, lemon juice, and 1½ teaspoons boiling water. Work until smooth, then transfer to a bowl. Season with salt and pepper to taste.
2 Devein the shrimp, rinse, and pat dry with paper towels. Heat the oil in a large skillet. Add the shrimp, garlic, and chili. Fry, stirring, over a medium heat for 4–5 minutes until the shrimp are cooked through.
3 Arrange the mozzarella and tomato slices on individual serving plates and top with the hot shrimp and their pan juices. Garnish with basil leaves and serve immediately, drizzled with the basil oil.

Note Mozzarella made from cow's milk can be used, but authentic buffalo mozzarella lends a superior flavor and texture.

Hot garlic shrimps are piled onto sliced tomatoes and buffalo mozzarella, then dressed with an emerald basil oil.

Vietnamese tamarind and shrimp soup

¾ pound small raw tiger shrimp

1½ pints vegetable stock

2 lemongrass stalks, roughly chopped

2 slices fresh galangal or gingerroot

2 shallots, diced

2 red chiles

2 ounces flat rice noodles

1 celery stick, sliced

1 tablespoon superfine sugar

1 tablespoon Thai fish sauce

2 tablespoons tamarind juice (see note)

1 tablespoon each chopped fresh cilantro, mint and basil

4 cooked shrimp in shells, to garnish

1 Remove, rinse, and reserve the heads and shells from the shrimp. Devein the shrimp and set aside. Put the shrimp shells and heads in a pan with the stock, lemongrass, galangal or ginger, shallots, and 1 whole chile. Bring to the boil, cover, and simmer gently for 30 minutes. Strain the flavored stock into a clean pan.

2 Put the noodles in a bowl, pour on boiling water, and then leave to soak for 5 minutes.

3 Meanwhile, seed and chop the remaining chile. Add to the stock with the shrimp, celery, sugar, fish sauce, and tamarind juice. Simmer gently for 2–3 minutes until the shrimp are cooked. Stir in the herbs.

4 Drain the noodles thoroughly, and divide between warm soup bowls. Spoon the soup over the noodles and garnish with the whole shrimp to serve.

Note Dried tamarind pulp is available from Indian food stores and some supermarkets. To make tamarind juice, dissolve 2 ounces tamarind pulp in ⅝ cup boiling water, then press through a sieve.

Smoked salmon parcels

Illustrated on previous pages

1 pound sliced smoked salmon
4 ounces cooked, peeled shrimp
6 ounces ricotta cheese
¼ cup crème fraîche
1 tablespoon chopped fresh chervil
1 tablespoon chopped fresh chives
1 tablespoon lemon juice

salt and pepper

For the garnish
salmon caviar
crème fraîche
chervil sprigs

To serve
toasted slices of brioche

1 Line 4 timbales or ramekins with the best smoked salmon slices, using about 10 ounces; allow sufficient overhang to cover the tops. Roughly chop the remaining smoked salmon.

2 Put the chopped salmon and shrimp in a food processor. Add the ricotta, crème fraîche, herbs, lemon juice, pepper, and a little salt; process until fairly smooth.

3 Spoon the ricotta mixture into the lined timbales or ramekins and spread evenly. Carefully fold the excess smoked salmon over the top to enclose the filling. Wrap the ramekins tightly with plastic wrap and chill in the refrigerator for several hours.

4 To serve, unmold the salmon mousses onto individual serving plates and garnish with a little extra crème fraîche, salmon caviar, and chervil sprigs. Serve with warm toasted brioche.

Jewel-like salmon eggs and crisp, toasted brioche elevate these simple parcels to a volumptuous appetizer.

Scallop, pancetta, and mushroom bruschetta

8 large scallops, cleaned
4 large thick slices good-quality white bread
1 garlic clove, peeled and halved
3–4 tbsp olive oil
2 ounces cubed pancetta or bacon cut crosswise into narrow strips
4 large flat mushrooms, cut into wedges
salt and pepper
2 tablespoons vinegar: sherry or balsamic

1 Cut away the tough muscle at the side of each scallop and any dark vein, then wash and dry. If the scallops are very large, halve them horizontally.
2 Toast the bread slices on both sides in the broiler, then rub with the garlic and drizzle with olive oil; keep warm.
3 Heat 2 tablespoons oil in a skillet, add the pancetta or bacon, and fry until beginning to brown. Increase the heat, add the scallops, and toss over a high heat for 2 minutes or until just opaque. Lift out with a slotted spoon and set aside.
4 Add the mushrooms, and fry for 2 minutes until softened, adding a little extra oil if needed.
5 Return the scallops to the pan, and stir over a high heat for a few seconds to warm through. Season well, then pile onto the warm bread. Deglaze the pan with the vinegar, and pour the juices over the scallops to serve.

Sautéed scallops, cubes of pancetta, and chunky mushrooms piled onto slices of toasted white bread rubbed with garlic and olive oil.

Mussels with coconut and cilantro pesto

32 large fresh mussels in shells
2 tablespoons freshly grated
   Parmesan
olive oil, for drizzling
For the pesto
handful fresh cilantro leaves

1 small garlic clove, crushed
2 tablespoons ground almonds
2 tablespoons coconut cream
2 tablespoons olive oil
pinch of cayenne pepper
salt and pepper

1 Scrub the mussels thoroughly in several changes of cold water and pull away any "beards" that are attached to the shells.

2 Put the mussels in a large pan, with just the water clinging to the shells after washing. Cover the pan with a tight-fitting lid and steam for 4 minutes until the shells have opened. Discard any that remain closed.

3 Refresh the mussels in cold water, drain well, and discard the empty half shells. Invert the mussels in their half shells on paper towels to drain thoroughly.

4 For the pesto, put all the ingredients in a food processor and work to a rough paste.

5 Place the mussels, open side up, in a broiler pan. Spoon a little pesto on top of each one, then sprinkle with the cheese. Drizzle with a little olive oil and grill for 3–4 minutes until bubbling and golden. Let cool for a minute or so before serving, with warm bread.

Note You can use ready-made basil pesto as a tasty, quick alternative to this coconut and cilantro pesto.

Mussels on their half shell are topped with a creamy coconut and cilantro pesto, then sprinkled with Parmesan and broiled.

Fish timbales with wasabi dressing

Serves 6

9 ounces skinless halibut or
   cod fillet
2 egg whites
1 pound skinless salmon or
   trout fillet
1⅛ cup heavy cream, chilled
salt and white pepper

For the dressing

6 teaspoons wasabi paste
6 teaspoons mirin (Japanese rice
   wine)
4 tablespoons rice wine vinegar
1 cup sunflower oil

For the garnish

8 ounces young spinach, shredded
oil for deep-frying

1 Mince the halibut in a food processor. Add a third of the egg white, a little at a time, mixing well between each addition. Transfer to a bowl. Repeat this process with the salmon, adding all of the remaining egg white. Chill both mixtures for 5 minutes.

2 Gradually stir a third of the cream into the halibut mixture; add the rest to the salmon, a little at a time. Season both mixtures.

3 Butter six ⅝-cup timbales, or other ovenproof molds. Divide half of the salmon mix between them. Cover with the halibut mixture, then top with the remaining salmon, to create layers. Chill for up to 3 hours.

4 For the dressing, shake the ingredients together in a screw-top jar to emulsify.

5 Heat the oil for deep-frying to 350°F. Fry the shredded spinach in batches for 15–20 seconds, until crisp but still bright green. Drain on paper towels.

6 Remove timbales from refrigerator 15 minutes before cooking. Preheat oven to 350°F. Stand the molds in a deep roasting pan and surround with a ⅛-inch depth of hot water. Cover with a dampened double layer of waxed paper. Bake for 15 minutes or until the tops are firm to the touch. Remove from pan and let stand, covered, for 10–15 minutes.

7 Unmold the timbales on paper towels, then lift onto plates. Top with the deep-fried spinach and drizzle the wasabi dressing around to serve.

A stylish, special-occasion starter.

Corn and coconut fritters

⅝ cup all-purpose flour
½ teaspoon baking powder
1 egg, lightly beaten
2 tablespoons coconut cream
1 tablespoon light soy sauce
1 tablespoon lemon juice
1¼ cup canned corn, drained
4 lime leaves, finely shredded
  (see note)

1 tablespoon chopped fresh cilantro
vegetable oil, for deep frying
For the dipping sauce
⅓ cup palm or superfine sugar
4 tablespoons rice wine vinegar
2 tablespoons Thai fish sauce
2 teaspoons chili sauce

1 First make the dipping sauce. Warm the ingredients together in a small pan to dissolve the sugar. Set aside to cool.
2 Sift the flour and baking powder into a bowl, and gradually beat in the egg, coconut cream, soy sauce, and lemon juice. Stir in the corn, lime leaves, and cilantro.
3 Heat a 2-inch depth of vegetable oil in a wok or deep, wide pan until it registers 350°F on a sugar thermometer. Drop in spoonfuls of the batter and fry in batches for 2–3 minutes until crisp and golden.
4 Drain on paper towels and keep warm in a low oven while cooking the rest of the fritters. Serve hot, with the dipping sauce.

Note Before shredding lime leaves, remove the thick central vein, which is often tough.

These fritters make a delicious appetizer or snack. Try serving them with iceberg lettuce and fresh herbs, such as cilantro and basil. To eat, roll the fritter and a few herb leaves in a lettuce leaf and dip into the sauce.

Warm artichoke and hazelnut salad

4 large globe artichokes, stalks
  removed
2 tablespoons extra-virgin olive oil
salt and pepper
6 ounces beans, trimmed
For the dressing
1 small garlic clove, crushed
4 tablespoons hazelnut oil
2 tablespoons extra virgin olive oil
1 tablespoon white wine vinegar
2 teaspoons wholegrain mustard
To serve
¼ cup hazelnuts, toasted and
  chopped
pecorino or Parmesan shavings

1 Put the artichokes in a large pan of cold water and bring to the boil.
Simmer, partially covered, for 20 minutes. Lift out and immediately plunge
into cold water; drain.

2 Trim away the artichoke leaves to reveal the heart. Using a spoon, scoop
out the prickly choke and discard. Toss the artichoke bases in olive oil and
season well.

3 Preheat a ridged grill or broiler pan. Cook the artichoke hearts for 5 minutes
each side, basting with oil, until tender. Cool slightly.

4 Meanwhile, whisk together the ingredients for the dressing, season to taste.

5 Cook the beans in boiling salted water for 3 minutes or until just tender;
drain well.

6 Lay the artichoke bases on warmed plates and arrange the beans on top.
Scatter the nuts and cheese shavings over. Serve drizzled with the dressing.

Freshly broiled globe artichokes, topped with
hot green beans and pecorino shavings, and
dressed with a hazelnut vinaigrette.

Asparagus with quail's eggs and prosciutto

Illustrated on previous pages

12 ounces thin asparagus spears, trimmed
1 tablespoon olive oil
salt and pepper
12 quail's eggs
4 slices prosciutto, or Parma ham

2 plum tomatoes, skinned, seeded, and diced

For the dressing
3 tablespoons extra virgin olive oil
2 teaspoons lemon juice
truffle oil, for drizzling (optional)

1 Peel the asparagus stalks, leaving the tips intact. Preheat a ridged grill pan. Brush the asparagus spears with olive oil and cook, turning, for 3–4 minutes, until tender and charred. Season lightly and set aside until cold.
2 Cook the quail's eggs in boiling water for 2 minutes; drain, and plunge into cold water. Once cool, peel and carefully halve the eggs.
3 Grill the prosciutto slices until crisp and golden; leave to cool, then break them in half.
4 For the dressing, whisk together the olive oil, lemon juice, and some salt and pepper.
5 To serve, arrange the asparagus, quail's eggs, and prosciutto slices on 4 large serving plates. Scatter the diced tomatoes over. Spoon the dressing over and add a generous drizzle of truffle oil, if using.

Grilling asparagus brings out the full, sweet flavor of this wonderful vegetable. Delicate quail's eggs (from specialist grocers) and crisp grilled pancetta are perfect partners.

Duck and mango salad with star anise

2 small duck breasts, each about
   ¼ pound
juice of ½ orange
1½ tablespoons dark soy sauce
1½ tablespoons clear honey
½ teaspoon ground cinnamon
¼ teaspoon ground star anise
4 ounces snow peas
¼ pound mixed salad leaves

1 small mango, peeled, stoned,
   and sliced
1 tablespoon sesame seeds, toasted
For the dressing
6 tablespoons peanut oil
4 teaspoons sesame oil
1½ tablespoons rice wine vinegar
2 tablespoons chopped fresh cilantro

1 Pat the duck breasts dry with paper towels, then score the fat. Lay them in a shallow dish. Mix the orange juice, soy sauce, honey, and spices together, pour over the duck and leave to marinate for 30 minutes.

2 Lift the duck breasts onto the grill rack, fat side down, reserving 2 tablespoons marinade. Grill for 2 minutes, then turn and grill for another 5–6 minutes, or until the duck is crisp on the outside but still slightly pink in the center. Cover loosely with foil and leave to rest in a warm place for 5 minutes.

3 Meanwhile, blanch the snow peas in lightly salted boiling water for 1 minute. Drain, refresh under cold water, and pat dry.

4 Whisk the dressing ingredients together in a bowl. Toss the salad leaves with a little of the dressing, and arrange on plates.

5 Put the reserved marinade and remaining dressing in a small pan. Bring to the boil; remove from heat.

6 Thinly slice the duck breasts and arrange on the salad leaves with the snow peas and mango slices. Drizzle the warm dressing over, and serve scattered with sesame seeds.

If you cannot buy ground star anise, grind whole ones to a powder in a spice grinder.

Grilled chicken and fig bruschetta

2 large chicken breast fillets (with skin)
2 tablespoons balsamic vinegar
1 teaspoon clear honey
2 tablespoons extra-virgin olive oil, plus extra for drizzling

salt and pepper
4 large, firm but ripe figs, halved
4 large slices rustic bread
1 peeled garlic clove, halved
4 slices prosciutto
handful of arugula leaves

1 Make several slashes through the skin side of each chicken breast. Mix together the balsamic vinegar, honey, oil, and seasoning. Set aside half of the mixture; brush the rest over the chicken and figs.

2 Heat a ridged grill pan or heavy-based skillet until smoking. Add the chicken and fry for 4–5 minutes each side until charred on the outside and cooked through. Lift out and leave to rest for 5 minutes. Add the figs to the pan, and cook for 1–2 minutes until softened.

3 Meanwhile, lightly toast the bread on both sides under the broiler, then rub all over with garlic and drizzle with olive oil; keep warm. Grill the prosciutto for about 1 minute each side until crisp.

4 Slice the chicken and arrange on the bruschetta with figs, prosciutto, and arugula leaves. Season and drizzle the remaining balsamic sauce over to serve.

Ridged grill pans give food an authentic chargrill flavor. Here, chicken and figs are bathed in a sweetened balsamic sauce, then grilled until charred and tender.

pasta

Pasta with gorgonzola, walnut, and herb sauce

2 slices wholewheat bread, crusts
    removed
¾ cup milk
2 cups walnut pieces
1 garlic clove, crushed
4½ ounces Gorgonzola cheese,
    in pieces

4 tablespoons extra-virgin olive oil
½ cup crème fraîche
6 tablespoons chopped fresh parsley
salt and pepper
1 pound dried ribbon pasta, such
    as pappardelle, tagliatelle, or
    fettucine

1 Preheat oven to 375°F. Soak the bread in the milk for 10 minutes or until all the milk is absorbed.

2 Spread the walnuts on a baking sheet and toast in the oven for 5 minutes. Transfer to a plate and allow to cool.

3 Put the soaked bread, walnuts, garlic, Gorgonzola, and olive oil in a food processor and process until almost smooth.

4 Transfer to a bowl, and stir in the crème fraîche and chopped parsley. Season generously with pepper, and a little salt if desired.

5 Bring a large pan of salted water to the boil. Add the pasta and cook until al dente. Drain, keeping back 2 tablespoons water in the pan. Immediately toss the pasta with the sauce. Cover with a lid and then leave to stand for 3 minutes before serving.

This creamy sauce relies on the heat of the cooked pasta to melt the cheese and warm the ingredients. The flavors develop on standing.

Walnut and mixed olive spaghetti

Serves 4–6

1½ cups (generous) mixed olives in extra-virgin olive oil

⅝ cup walnuts (ideally freshly shelled)

juice of ½ orange (3–4 tbsp)

1 pound 2 ounces dried wholewheat spaghetti

salt and pepper (black or five-pepper mix)

freshly grated Parmesan cheese, to serve

1 Strain the olives and reserve the oil. Stone and slice the olives. Grate the walnuts, using a mouli grater or food processor.

2 For the dressing, mix together the orange juice and olive oil.

3 Cook the spaghetti in a large pan of boiling salted water until al dente. Return to the warm pan and add the olive slices, grated walnuts, dressing, and seasoning; toss lightly together. Serve at once, with grated Parmesan and a salad.

Olives give this sauce such a superb flavor that stoning them is worth the effort.

Fusilli lunghi, peppers, and anchovy olives

3 tablespoons olive oil

1 large onion, thinly sliced

3 garlic cloves, thinly sliced

2 red bell peppers, cored, seeded, and sliced

3 zucchini, cut into sticks

two 5-ounce cans peeled tomatoes in rich juice

2 tablespoons chopped fresh basil

salt and pepper

10 ounces dried fusilli lunghi, or lasagnette

¾ cup anchovy-stuffed olives, halved

For the topping

8-ounce tub mascarpone cheese

2 ounces Parmesan cheese, coarsely grated

¼ cup pine nuts

basil leaves, to garnish

1 Heat the oil in a large skillet and fry the onion until golden. Add the garlic, peppers, and zucchini, and stir-fry over a high heat for 5 minutes.

2 Stir in the tomatoes with their juice and the chopped basil. Season and simmer gently for 10 minutes until the vegetables are tender.

3 Meanwhile, cook the pasta in a large pan of boiling salted water until al dente. Drain the pasta and refresh under cold running water; drain again.

4 Stir the pasta into the tomato mixture with the olives. Turn into a large ovenproof dish, and top with mascarpone. Sprinkle with the Parmesan cheese and pine nuts. (If preparing ahead, cover with plastic wrap and chill.)

5 To serve, preheat the oven to 400°F. Bake the pasta dish for 30 minutes or until bubbling. Let stand for a few minutes, then scatter with basil leaves and serve with crusty bread.

Note For a vegetarian dish, use olives stuffed with pimientos instead of anchovies.

Anchovy olives provide a piquant flavor, while mascarpone and Parmesan melt to an irresistible creamy topping.

Pappardelle with sun-dried tomato sauce

Illustrated on previous pages

Serves 4–6

⅔ cup sun-dried eggplant slices (see note)

3 garlic cloves, peeled

4 tablespoons sun-dried tomato paste

2¼ cups grilled artichoke hearts in olive oil (see note)

salt and pepper

1 pound 2 ounces dried pappardelle

4 tbsp roughly torn fresh parsley

⅓ cup pine nuts, toasted

1 Simmer sun-dried eggplants in water to cover for 2 minutes. Drain and refresh in cold water; dry on paper towels. Cut each slice into 3 long strips.
2 Simmer garlic in water to cover for 7–8 minutes until softened. Drain and crush garlic with the back of a knife, then mix with sun-dried tomato paste.
3 Drain the artichokes, reserving 4 tablespoons oil; halve any larger ones. Heat the reserved oil in a large skillet, and stir-fry the eggplants until cooked. Add artichokes and heat through. Add garlic mixture and season; keep warm.
4 Cook the pasta in a large pan of boiling salted water until al dente. Add 4 tablespoons of the cooking liquid to the sauce. Drain the pasta, and toss with the hot sauce, parsley, and pine nuts to serve.

Note Chargrilled sun-dried eggplants and grilled artichoke hearts in oil are sold in some delicatessens and supermarkets. Alternatively, substitute 1 large fresh eggplant, thinly sliced, and a jar of artichoke hearts in oil, drained. Brush the eggplant slices with oil, and grill on both sides until charred. Fry the artichokes in 2 tablespoons olive oil until tinged brown. Add both to the sauce.

This delicious sauce can be made in advance and reheated as the pasta is cooking.

Tortelloni with creamy dolcelatte sauce

1 pound 2 ounces dried tortelloni
salt and pepper
4 tablespoons butter
5 ounces dolcelatte cheese, cut into
  small cubes

¾ cup heavy cream
3 ounces Parmesan cheese, finely
  grated
chopped flat-leaf parsley, to garnish

1 Cook the tortelloni according to packet instructions or until al dente.
2 Meanwhile, melt the butter in a small, heavy-based pan over a low heat.
Add the dolcelatte and stir until completely melted. Add the cream, and
slowly bring to a simmer, stirring. When the sauce is thick enough to coat
the spoon, stir in the Parmesan. Season to taste.
3 Drain the tortelloni and toss with the sauce. Serve sprinkled with chopped
parsley and accompanied by a salad.

This is excellent with any bought tortelloni.
The dolcelatte must be young, not aged.

Herb and parmesan pasta

For the pasta

1⅛ cup semolina flour, for pasta

¾ ounce Parmesan cheese, finely grated

2 medium eggs (preferably organic, for yolk color)

48 flat leaf parsley leaves, stalks removed

1 To make the pasta, put all the ingredients in a food processor, and pulse until the mixture forms lumpy grains. Tip onto a lightly floured surface (not marble) and knead together until smooth. Wrap in plastic wrap and refrigerate for at least 3 hours.

2 Cut the pasta into manageable portions; keep wrapped. Roll out, one piece at a time, using a pasta machine. Pass dough through the widest setting at least 3 times, then gradually narrow the setting as you roll out, until you have a thin, pliable sheet of pasta.

3 Lay parsley leaves on one pasta sheet at 1-inch intervals, and then place another sheet of pasta on top to sandwich the leaves. Roll through the machine on a medium setting, then once through on a narrow setting. Cut into rectangles around the leaves, with a pasta wheel or a knife. Leave to dry slightly on waxed paper for 3 hours (or overnight).

4 Add the pasta to a large pan of boiling salted water with 2 tablespoons oil; cook for 3–4 minutes, until al dente. Serve with your favourite pasta sauce.

Parsley leaves are sandwiched between layers of homemade pasta to stunning effect. A fresh tomato sauce is the ideal complement.

Pasta with arugula and red bell pepper sauce

Serves 4–6

For the sauce

8 tablespoons extra-virgin olive oil

2 onions, minced

4 red bell peppers, halved, cored, and
seeded

salt and pepper

To finish

3 tablespoons oil

¼ pound arugula leaves

1 To make the sauce, heat 4 tablespoons of the oil in a heavy-based skillet, and gently fry the onions over a low heat for 10 minutes, turning occasionally. Broil the peppers until charred, let cool slightly, then skin. Dice the pepper flesh and add to the onions with the remaining oil. Cook on a low heat for 20 minutes until soft, but not brown.

2 Add the pasta to a large pan of boiling salted water with 2 tablespoons oil, and cook for 3–4 minutes until al dente: allow 3–4 minutes for fresh pasta; longer for dried pasta (refer to packet instructions). Meanwhile, heat 1 tablespoon oil in a large pan, add the arugula, and cook briefly until just wilted. Drain the pasta and serve at once on the wilted arugula, topped with the hot sauce.

Parsley leaves are sandwiched between layers of homemade pasta and served in a vivid pepper sauce with arugula.

Pasta with roast peppers and shallots

2 red bell peppers
8 shallots, thickly sliced
4 tablespoons olive oil
1 pound dried chunky pasta shapes,
  such as rigatoni or shells

salt and pepper
2 tablespoons balsamic vinegar
freshly grated Parmesan cheese,
  to serve

1 Preheat oven to 400°F. Place the whole red peppers and sliced shallots in a small roasting pan and drizzle with the oil. Turn the peppers and shallots to coat with the oil.

2 Roast in the oven for 10–15 minutes until the shallots are golden brown. Using a slotted spoon, transfer the shallots to a saucepan.

3 Roast the peppers, turning occasionally, for another 15–20 minutes until charred. Leave until cool enough to handle, then skin. Halve the peppers, discard the seeds, and cut the flesh into strips. Add the pepper strips and any juices to the shallots.

4 Bring a large pan of salted water to the boil. Add the pasta and cook until al dente.

5 Meanwhile, reheat the shallot mixture and stir in the balsamic vinegar. Cook over a high heat for 1 minute. Season with salt and pepper to taste.

6 Drain the pasta, keeping back 2 tablespoons water in the pan. Immediately toss with the sauce. Serve accompanied by freshly grated Parmesan.

For a treat, serve topped with a dollop of creamy mascarpone flavored with cracked black peppercorns.

Lemon pasta salad with mushrooms

Illustrated on previous pages

Serves 3–4; or 6 as part of a meal

1 tablespoon olive oil

12 ounces flat mushrooms, cut into
wedges

1 teaspoon coriander seeds, crushed

2 teaspoons finely chopped fresh sage

½ teaspoon grated lemon zest

3 tablespoons lemon juice

9 ounces fresh ballerine or farfalle
pasta

salt and pepper

sage leaves, to garnish

1 Heat the oil in a skillet and stir-fry the mushrooms for 2–3 minutes, then
add the coriander and sage. Cook for 2–3 minutes until the mushroom juices
start to run. Remove from the heat and add the lemon zest and juice.
2 Add the pasta to a large pan of boiling salted water and cook for a few
minutes only, until al dente. Drain, refresh in cold water and drain well.
3 Toss the warm mushrooms and pasta together. Season with salt and
pepper to taste. Serve garnished with sage.

Variation Replace the mushrooms with 3 red or orange bell peppers,
skinned, seeded, and sliced.

This tangy pasta salad is best served freshly
made, while it is still warm.

Pasta salad with olives, peppers, and artichokes

2 large red or orange bell peppers
2 garlic cloves, peeled
1⅛ cup dried pasta shapes, such as
  spirals or shells
1⅛ cup marinated broiled artichoke
  hearts in olive oil (see note)
generous ¼ cup pitted black olives

1 tablespoon capers, drained
2 tablespoons chopped fresh flat leaf
  parsley
For the dressing
1 tablespoon balsamic vinegar
3 tablespoons extra-virgin olive oil
salt and pepper

1 Put the peppers, skin-side up, on the broiler rack with the unpeeled garlic cloves (for the dressing). Broil under a medium-high heat, turning from time to time, until the pepper skins are blistered and charred. Set aside the garlic for the dressing. Put the broiled peppers in a bowl, cover tightly with plastic wrap, and leave to cool slightly.

2 Peel away the skins from the peppers, then halve, core, and deseed, reserving the juices. Cut the peppers into strips.

3 For the dressing, squeeze the garlic flesh from the skins into a bowl, and add the balsamic vinegar and olive oil. Whisk to combine, and season with salt and pepper.

4 Cook the pasta in a large pan of boiling, salted water until al dente. Drain, then refresh under cold running water and drain thoroughly. Tip the pasta into a large bowl, add the dressing, and toss to mix.

5 Drain and slice the artichoke hearts. Add to the pasta with the broiled pepper strips, olives, and capers. Cover and leave to stand at room temperature for an hour or so before serving, to allow the flavors to develop.

6 Add chopped parsley to the salad, and check the seasoning before serving

Note If you cannot buy broiled artichoke hearts, use a jar of artichoke hearts in olive oil instead.

Saffron pasta

Makes 12 ounces
¼ teaspoon saffron strands
2 eggs (preferably organic,
 for yolk color)

scant 8¼ cups semolina flour,
 for pasta
extra flour, for dusting

1 Crush the saffron strands, using a mortar and pestle, add the eggs, and then mix well.
2 Put the egg mixture into a food processor, add the flour, and pulse until the mixture forms lumpy grains.
3 Turn onto a lightly floured surface (not marble, as this is too cold), and knead until smooth. Wrap in plastic wrap and leave to rest in the refrigerator for at least 3 hours.
4 Use a pasta machine to roll the dough into thin sheets to make ravioli, or for tagliatelle or spaghetti, fit the appropriate cutters to the machine after rolling. Cook in boiling salted water, until al dente, allowing 3–4 minutes for ribbon pasta; 4–6 minutes for ravioli. Serve with your favourite sauce.

Variations
Sun-dried tomato pasta Replace the saffron with a generous ⅛ cup chopped sun-dried tomatoes (not in oil). Process to a purée with the eggs.
Mushroom pasta Replace the saffron with ¾ cup dried porcini, ground to a powder.
Spinach pasta Wilt ¼ pound spinach in 1 tablespoon oil, drain well and squeeze out all moisture. Purée in the processor with the eggs.

Note For convenience, you can make the pasta 1–2 days in advance. Keep tightly wrapped in plastic wrap, refrigerated, until required. If you are making ravioli, prepare these a day ahead, freeze overnight, and cook from frozen. (They are best frozen for a short time only.)

Satisfying to prepare—and not too difficult—homemade pasta is well worth the effort.

Saffron ravioli with butternut squash

Also illustrated on following pages

1 pound 10 ounces butternut
 squash, quartered
4 tablespoons sunflower oil
salt and pepper
2¼ ounces pecorino or Parmesan
 cheese, grated
1 quantity saffron pasta dough
1 egg white

For the dressing
4 garlic cloves, thinly sliced
⅝ cup extra-virgin olive oil
⅝ cup black olives, stoned and sliced
4 teaspoons fresh thyme leaves,
 roughly chopped
3 ounces pecorino or Parmesan
 cheese

1 Preheat oven to 400°F. Place squash quarters on a baking sheet and drizzle
with oil; season. Roast for 55 minutes until very soft. Discard seeds; scoop
flesh into a food processor. Add cheese and ⅛ teaspoon pepper, and purée.
2 Cut the pasta into manageable portions; keep wrapped. Roll out, one piece
at a time, using a pasta machine. Pass dough through the widest setting at
least 3 times, then gradually narrow the setting until you have a thin, pliable
sheet. Pass through thinnest setting 3 times. Repeat with remaining dough.
3 Place a pasta sheet on a board, and stamp out disks, with a 2½-inch fluted
cutter. Lay half the disks on a sheet of plastic wrap and paint edges with egg
white. Put a teaspoon of squash filling in the center of each, and top with
the other disks, sticking the edges together without squashing the filling.
4 Repeat with the rest of the pasta to make about 35 ravioli. Place on trays
lined with plastic wrap, spacing apart. Freeze or use within 1 hour.
5 To make the dressing, put garlic and oil in a small pan, and heat gently until
beginning to turn golden. Add olives, thyme, and pepper. Set aside to infuse.
6 When ready to serve, bring a large saucepan of salted water to the boil, and
add 2 tablesppons oil. Cook ravioli for 4–6 minutes until al dente; drain. Serve
the ravioli with warm dressing poured over, and top with pecorino shavings.

Homemade ravioli served with a warm
dressing of garlic, olives, and thyme.

Fettucine with asparagus and pancetta

¼ teaspoon saffron threads

5 ounces pancetta, diced

1 pound asparagus

1 pound dried spinach fettucine

salt and pepper

6 tablespoons butter

4 green onions, thinly sliced

½ cup dry white wine

1 cup heavy cream

3 tablespoons snipped fresh chives

2 ounces Parmesan cheese, finely grated

1 Soak the saffron in 2 tablespoons hot water.

2 Preheat a heavy-based skillet, then add the pancetta and fry, stirring, until golden and crisp. Set aside.

3 Cut asparagus into short lengths, keeping the tips whole. Parboil for 5 minutes; drain.

4 Cook the fettucine in a large pan of boiling salted water until al dente.

5 Meanwhile, melt the butter in a large skillet. Add the green onions and cook for 1 minute, then add the asparagus and sauté for 1–2 minutes. Pour in the wine and cook for 3 minutes. Stir in the cream, saffron, and soaking liquid. Bring to a simmer.

6 Drain the pasta and add to the saffron sauce with the chives, Parmesan, and pancetta. Toss well, season, and serve.

Spinach flavored tagliatelle, tossed in a creamy saffron sauce with fresh asparagus, green onions, pancetta, and chives.

Seafood spaghetti

Serves 4–6

2¼ pounds mussels in shells, cleaned
250g/9oz peeled, raw tiger shrimp
2 tablespoons butter
⅜ cup white wine
1 teaspoon finely grated lemon zest
2 teaspoons mild curry paste
1¼ cup light cream
6 ounces smoked salmon trimmings, sliced
salt and pepper
1 pound 2 ounces dried spaghetti
lemon wedges, to serve

1 Discard damaged mussels or any open ones that do not close when tapped sharply. Halve the shrimp lengthwise and devein.

2 Melt the butter in a large pan with the wine and 4 tablespoons water. Add the mussels, cover tightly, and cook briskly for 4 minutes, or until the shells open, shaking the pan from time to time. Discard any mussels that have not opened.

3 Lift out the mussels with a slotted spoon; set aside 12 for the garnish. Remove the rest of the mussels from their shells.

4 Add the shrimp to the pan. Cook, stirring, for 4–5 minutes until they turn pink. Stir in the lemon zest, curry paste, and cream, then add the smoked salmon and shelled mussels. Heat through gently and season with salt and pepper to taste.

5 Meanwhile, cook the spaghetti in a large pan of boiling salted water until al dente. Drain and toss with the seafood sauce. Serve immediately, garnished with the reserved mussels and accompanied by lemon wedges.

Note Always add pasta to a large saucepan containing plenty of boiling water. Cook at a fast boil to prevent sticking.

Serve this luxurious pasta dish with a leafy green salad, dressed with lemon juice and light olive oil.

Seafood pasta with a coconut cream sauce

½ cup heavy cream

½ cup coconut milk

1–2 tablespoons sun-dried tomato paste

1 pound dried spinach tagliatelle, smoked salmon tagliatelle, or egg pappardelle

salt and pepper

1 tablespoon olive oil

3 green onions, thinly sliced

1 garlic clove, crushed

1 teaspoon grated fresh gingerroot

1 red chile, seeded and finely chopped

10 ounces cooked peeled tiger shrimp

1¼ cup white crabmeat

3 tablespoons chopped fresh cilantro leaves

cilantro leaves, to garnish

1 In a bowl, whisk together the cream, coconut milk, and sun-dried tomato paste; set aside.

2 Cook the pasta in a large pan of boiling salted water until al dente.

3 Meanwhile, heat the oil in a large pan. Add the green onions, garlic, ginger, and chile. Stir-fry for 2 minutes, then add the shrimp and crabmeat. Heat through, stirring, for 1 minute.

4 Add the cream mixture and slowly bring to a simmer, stirring. Add the chopped cilantro, stir well, and season with salt and pepper to taste.

5 Drain the pasta and toss with the seafood sauce. Serve immediately, scattered with cilantro leaves.

A delicious fusion of shrimp and crabmeat, flavored with green onions, chile and cilantro in a coconut cream sauce.

Squid ink pasta with a spicy seafood sauce

3 tablespoons extra-virgin olive oil
4 garlic cloves, finely chopped
1 pound dried squid ink pasta
salt and pepper
10 ounces cleaned baby squid, cut
  into rings
10 ounces raw tiger shrimp, peeled
  and deveined

1–2 red chiles, seeded and finely
  sliced
⅝ cup dry white wine
15-ounce can chopped tomatoes
3 tablespoons chopped flat-leaf
  parsley
flat-leaf parsley sprigs, to garnish

1 Heat the oil in a large, heavy-based skillet and gently sauté the garlic until softened.
2 Meanwhile, cook the pasta in a large pan of boiling salted water until al dente.
3 Add the squid and shrimp to the garlic. Stir-fry over a high heat for 2–3 minutes, then add the chilli and wine. Lower heat to medium and cook for 3–4 minutes. Add the tomatoes and parsley and cook for another 3–4 minutes. Season to taste.
4 Drain the pasta, toss with the seafood sauce, and then serve, garnished with some parsley.

Squid, tiger shrimp, chile, tomatoes, wine, and a hint of garlic are a combined with black squid ink pasta for a dramatic dish.

Individual salmon lasagne

Illustrated on previous pages

3¾ cups milk
6 tablespoons butter
⅝ cup all-purpose flour
1 fresh bay leaf
salt and pepper
2 tablespoons creamed horseradish
squeeze of lemon juice (optional)

1 pound 2 ounces boneless, skinless
  salmon fillets, cut into small cubes
8 sheets dried (no need to pre-cook)
  lasagne
6 smoked salmon slices
For the topping
3 ounces Emmental cheese, grated

1 Pour the milk into a pan. Add the butter, flour, bay leaf, and seasoning. Whisk over a medium heat, until the sauce is smooth and thickened.

2 Pour half the sauce into a bowl, and add horseradish with a squeeze of lemon juice. Stir in salmon cubes. Leave the bay leaf in remaining sauce, to infuse.

3 Parboil the lasagne in a large pan of boiling salted water with 2 tablespoons oil added for 5 minutes (to shorten the baking time).

4 Spoon a third of the salmon mix into the base of four individual pie dishes, cover with a sheet of lasagne, then spoon the rest of the salmon mix over.

5 Cover with the remaining lasagne sheets, and top with a slice of smoked salmon. Discard the bay leaf, then spoon the sauce over the smoked salmon.

6 Halve the other 2 smoked salmon slices, and place one on each portion. Scatter with the cheese. If preparing ahead, cover and chill for up to 24 hours.

7 To serve, preheat oven to 375°F. Bake the lasagnes for 30 minutes until bubbling. If necessary, brown under the broiler. Serve with a fennel, baby spinach, and orange salad.

Freezing If frozen salmon isn't used, lasagnes may be frozen before baking.

Creamed horseradish marries this flavor combination of fresh and smoked salmon perfectly. Avoid overcooking the lasagne.

Flounder- and caper-stuffed conchiglioni

9 ounces dried conchiglioni
(about 40 very large, unbroken
pasta shells)
salt and pepper
1 pound 2 ounces flounder fillet,
skinned

2 cups vegetable stock
1 large or 2 small fennel bulbs,
thinly sliced
1 tablespoon capers, rinsed
2 tablespoons butter, chilled

1 Preheat oven to 350°F. Cook the pasta shells in a large pan of boiling
salted water until al dente. Drain and immediately rinse in cold water; drain.
2 Heat the stock in a pan, add the fennel, and poach for 15 minutes until
tender. Drain and spread in a shallow ovenproof dish.
3 Cut the flounder into about 40 pieces and pop one piece into each pasta
shell. Place the shells, stuffed side up, on top of the fennel. Sprinkle with
the capers and season generously with pepper. Place a tiny dot of butter
in each shell.
4 Cover the dish with foil and bake for 30 minutes or until the fish is opaque.

Variation Bake the stuffed pasta shells on a bed of thinly sliced fresh
tomatoes instead of poached fennel. You will need 4 large tomatoes.

Chunks of fish nestling in large pasta shells
on a bed of sweet, poached fennel. Assemble
1–2 hours in advance, and bake as required.

Corn spaghetti with squid and salmon

Serves 6

3-inch piece fresh gingerroot, peeled

oil for deep-frying

1¼ pound salmon fillet, skinned and
cut into 1-inch pieces

2 tablespoons olive oil

salt and pepper

¾ pound baby squid, cleaned and cut
into ½-inch pieces

1 pound 2 ounces dried corn
spaghetti

For the dressing

⅝ cup olive oil

3 tablespoons dry white wine

2 tablespoons lemon juice

2 tablespoons chopped fresh dill

For the garnish

dill sprigs

1 Finely slice the ginger lengthwise, then cut into fine julienne strips.
Heat a 2-inch depth of oil in a deep pan to 325°F. Deep-fry the ginger until
golden. Drain on paper towels.

2 Toss the salmon in 1 tablespoon oil; season well. Repeat with the squid.
Heat oven to 325°F.

3 Heat a non-stick skillet until very hot. Add the salmon and sear for
30 seconds each side. Remove and keep warm in a covered dish in the oven.
Repeat with squid.

4 Add the spaghetti to a large pan of boiling salted water and cook until
al dente.

5 Meanwhile, whisk the dressing ingredients together, except the dill, in
a pan; warm through.

6 Drain the pasta well and place in a bowl. Add the chopped dill and
dressing; toss well. Fold in the salmon and squid.

7 Top with dill sprigs, a generous grinding of pepper, and the ginger
julienne to serve.

Corn pasta has a wonderful color and looks
great with pink salmon.

All-in-one curried noodles

6 ounces rice stick or egg thread
noodles
1 tablespoon sunflower oil
1 red bell pepper, cored, seeded,
and cut into thin sticks
1 red onion, cut into wedges
¼ pound baby corncobs, halved
lengthwise
¼ pound sugar snap peas, halved

¼ pound closed cap mushrooms,
halved
2 tablespoons madras curry paste
15-ounce can coconut milk
2 tablespoons light soy sauce
7 ounces extra large cooked tiger
shrimp (thawed and dried if frozen)
4 tablespoons chopped fresh cilantro
cilantro sprigs, to garnish

1 Put the noodles in a bowl, pour on boiling water, and leave to soak for
5 minutes or according to packet directions.
2 Heat the oil in a large skillet or wok. Add the red pepper and onion, and
stir-fry for a few minutes until starting to soften.
3 Toss in the baby corn and stir-fry for 2 minutes, then add the sugar snap
peas and mushrooms, and stir-fry for another few minutes.
4 Stir in the curry paste, then pour in the coconut milk and soy sauce. Add
the shrimp and chopped cilantro; toss well. Divide the noodles between
warmed bowls, add the curried sauce, and serve garnished with cilantro.

Tiger shrimp tossed with noodles and plenty
of vegetables in a curried coconut sauce.

Penne with meatballs in tomato sauce

For the meatballs
1 pound lean ground beef
grated zest of ½ lemon
1 teaspoon ground coriander
½ teaspoon ground cumin
2 tablespoons chopped fresh oregano
1 tablespoon chopped fresh cilantro
  or parsley
1 tablespoon harissa paste

⅜ cup fresh white breadcrumbs
1 small egg, beaten
salt and pepper
1 tablespoon olive oil
For the sauce and pasta
1 shallot, finely chopped
1 garlic clove, crushed
1⅛ cup carton passata (see note)
2 tablespoons chopped fresh parsley

1 To prepare the meatballs, put the ground beef in a bowl with the lemon zest, spices, herbs, harissa paste, and breadcrumbs. Season generously with salt and pepper, and mix together, using your hands until evenly blended. Work in the beaten egg to bind, then shape the mixture into about 30 small balls.
2 Heat the olive oil in a large skillet, add the meatballs, and fry over medium heat, turning to brown evenly, for about 5 minutes. Remove with a slotted spoon, and drain off all but 1 tablespoon fat from the pan.
3 Add the shallots and garlic to the pan, and fry gently for about 5 minutes until beginning to soften. Add the passata and bring to a simmer, then season well with salt and pepper. Return the meatballs to the pan and simmer, partially covered, for 15 minutes, until cooked through.
4 In the meantime, cook the pasta in a large pan of boiling salted water until al dente. Drain and return to the pan. Add 3–4 tablespoons of the sauce from the meatballs, and toss to mix.
5 Divide the pasta among warmed plates, top with the meatballs in tomato sauce, and scatter with the chopped parsley to serve.

Flavoured with oregano, harissa, cumin, and cilantro, these tasty meatballs are delicious served with pasta and a simple tomato sauce.

Caserecce gratin with taleggio and prosciutto

Serves 6

2 cups milk

scant ¼ cup all-purpose flour

2 tablespoons butter

salt and pepper

freshly grated nutmeg

2 tablespoons sunflower oil

¾ pound young leaf spinach

1 pound 2 ounces dried caserecce,
  or spirals

5 ounces prosciutto, cut into strips

½ pound taleggio cheese, finely diced

1 Preheat oven to 400°F. Grease a 10 x 8-inch gratin dish.

2 Place the milk, flour, and butter in a heavy-based pan over a medium heat and whisk until thick. Season with pepper, nutmeg, and a little salt.

3 Heat the oil in a large wok or other pan, add spinach, and cook over a high heat for 1 minute only, turning continuously. Transfer to a colander and drain.

4 Add the pasta to a large pan of boiling salted water. Cook for 2 minutes less than the time suggested on the packet. Drain well and tip into the gratin dish.

5 Add the spinach, prosciutto, two-thirds of the cheese, and the sauce. Season with pepper. Toss well. Dot the surface with the remaining cheese, and dust with nutmeg.

6 Cover with foil and bake for 10 minutes. Uncover and bake for another 5 minutes.

Note For convenience, make in advance. Keep covered in the fridge, but bring to room temperature before baking, allowing an extra 10 minutes in the oven.

A slightly twisted pasta, caserecce is ideal for gratins. Taleggio has a delicious tang, though gruyère may be used.

fish

Shrimp on crackling rice pancakes

packet (approx. 9 ounces) instant
   risotto, preferably saffron flavored
1 garlic clove, finely chopped
¾-inch piece fresh gingerroot, peeled
   and grated
2 tablespoons chopped fresh chives
4 green onions, finely chopped

salt and pepper
1 pound 10 ounces medium raw
   shrimp in shells
2 tablespoons butter
2 tablespoons sunflower oil
2 tablespoons Thai red curry paste
chives, to garnish

1 To make the risotto, cook the rice according to the packet instructions,
together with the garlic, ginger, chives, green onions, and seasoning. Tip
onto a tray; allow to cool. When cold, shape into 8 cakes, with wet hands.
2 Shell the shrimp, leaving the tail shells on.
3 Melt the butter in a skillet and cook the pancakes carefully, a few
at a time, until golden and crisp on one side; turn and cook the other side.
Avoid moving during cooking, or they might break up. Keep warm.
4 Heat the oil in a wok or skillet, add the curry paste, and cook, stirring,
for 1 minute. Add the shrimp and stir-fry for 3–4 minutes until cooked.
Serve at once, on the rice cakes. Garnish with chives.

An impressive dish to rustle up from the
pantry, using instant risotto rice.

Deep-fried shrimp with harissa salsa

Serves 3–4

24 large raw shrimp

1¾ cup well seasoned fish stock

pinch each of turmeric and chile powder

1¼ cup couscous

8 tablespoons chopped cilantro leaves

2 red chiles, seeded and finely diced

salt and pepper

oil for deep-frying

seasoned flour, for coating

2 eggs, beaten

For the harissa salsa

2 garlic cloves, crushed

1 teaspoon ground coriander

2 teaspoons ground caraway seeds

2 teaspoons mild chile powder (preferably Ancho)

1 teaspoon sugar

1 tomato, seeded and finely diced

¼ cup olive oil

juice of 1 lemon

For the garnish

deep-fried flat leaf parsley

1 Shell and devein the shrimp, leaving the tail shells on; set aside.

2 Next, prepare the harissa salsa. Mash the garlic with the spices and a little salt, stir in the remaining ingredients, and set aside.

3 For the shrimp coating, bring the stock to the boil, and add the turmeric and chile powder. Pour over the couscous, cover, and leave until the liquid is absorbed. When cool enough to handle, break up the couscous. Add the cilantro and chiles; season well.

4 Heat oil for deep-frying to 310°F Dip the shrimp into seasoned flour, then egg, then coat with couscous. Deep-fry, a few at a time, for 3–4 minutes until cooked; drain on paper towels. Serve garnished with fried parsley and accompanied by the salsa.

Spicy couscous-coated shrimp.

Seafood with pine nuts and garlic

Serves 4–6

¼ cup raisins
¼ cup brandy
3 garlic cloves, crushed
1 cup pine nuts, lightly toasted
salt and pepper
6 tablespoons olive oil
1 large onion, minced
8 tomatoes, skinned and chopped

2 teaspoons paprika
4 fresh bay leaves
½ cup dry white wine
30 mussels in shells, cleaned
24 clams in shells, cleaned (optional)
8–12 whole large raw shrimp
1½ pounds thick cod fillet, cut into
  2-inch chunks
8–12 small new potatoes, cooked

1 Soak the raisins in the brandy for 1 hour. Mash the garlic and two-thirds of the pine nuts to a paste with a little salt.

2 Heat 3 tablespoons oil in a heavy-based pan, and gently fry the onion until soft. Increase the heat and add the tomatoes, paprika, bay leaves, seasoning, and wine. Stir well until beginning to thicken. Transfer to a bowl.

3 Bring 1¾ cup salted water to the boil in a large pan. Add mussels, and clams, if using. Cover and shake the pan over a medium heat for about 4 minutes, until the shells open. Drain, reserving the liquor; discard any unopened ones. Strain the liquor; stir a little into the garlic paste.

4 Heat the remaining oil in a deep pan, and sauté the shrimp for 1 minute. Add the raisins and brandy, and cook for 1 minute. Stir in the tomato mix.

5 Add the remaining liquor to the pan, and bring to a gentle simmer, then remove the shrimp with a slotted spoon. Add the cod to the pan and cook for 5 minutes; remove. Increase the heat, then add the garlic paste and potatoes. Simmer for a few minutes.

6 To serve, add all of the seafood to the pan and heat through gently. Sprinkle with the remaining pine nuts.

This rich Spanish stew is substantial enough to serve as a meal in itself. Accompany with plenty of flat bread to mop up the tasty juices.

Salmon with anchovies and capers

Serves 4–6

3¼–3½ pound whole salmon

8 anchovy fillets

1 tablespoon capers

2–3 tablespoons fresh parsley

1 teaspoon grated lemon rind

juice of ½ lemon

pepper, to season

1 Preheat oven to 425°F. Clean the salmon and make 4 or 5 diagonal slits on each side of it.

2 Finely chop the anchovy fillets, capers, and fresh parsley. Mix together with the grated lemon rind and the lemon juice.

3 Press this paste into the cuts in the fish. Season with pepper, wrap in oiled foil, and seal loosely. Bake for 45 minutes.

4 Leave, wrapped, to rest and finish cooking in its own steam for 15 minutes.

Piquant whole baked salmon.

Roasted monkfish with saffron aioli

Illustrated on previous pages

Serves 4–6

2 small monkfish tails, each
    1¼ pounds, filleted and skinned
    (i.e. 4 fillets in total)
salt and pepper
4 fresh rosemary srigs
4–6 lemon slices
2 tablespoons olive oil

For the marinade

4 garlic cloves, crushed
1½ teaspoons finely chopped fresh
    rosemary
1½ teaspoons ground coriander

1½ teaspoons ground cumin
2 teaspoons sweet paprika
4 tablespoons finely chopped fresh
    cilantro leaves
2 tablespoons white wine
4 tablespoons olive oil

For the saffron aioli

2 garlic cloves
pinch of saffron strands
1 egg yolk
⅞ cup oz olive oil
2 tablespoons lemon juice
    (approximately)

1 To make the marinade, pound the garlic, 1 teaspoon salt and the rosemary to a paste, using a pestle and mortar. Add the remaining ingredients; mix well. Refrigerate.

2 To make the aioli, pound garlic, saffron, and ¼ teaspoon salt to a paste, then place in a blender with egg yolk. With the motor runnin, slowly add the oil through the feeder tube until the aioli is thick. Transfer to a bowl, and stir in lemon juice. Cover and chill.

3 To prepare the monkfish, smear the flat side of two fillets with the marinade, and sandwich together with the other fillets. Tie at intervals with cotton string, and place in a shallow dish. Leave to marinate in a cool place for 2–3 hours.

4 To cook, preheat oven to 425°F. Place the fish on a rack in a roasting pan and season well. Thread the rosemary sprigs and lemon slices through the string. Drizzle with the 2 tablespoons oil, and roast for 20 minutes or until cooked through.

5 Leave the fish to rest for 5–10 minutes before serving, with the saffron aioli and French fries.

Skate with nutty brown butter

½ red onion, minced

6 tablespoons cider vinegar

4 cleaned skate wings, each about
  7 ounces

7 cups court bouillon (see note)

1 teaspoon yellow mustard seeds

4 tablespoons unsalted butter

4 tablespoons finely chopped fresh
  parsley

caper berries or capers, to garnish

1 Put the chopped red onion into a small bowl, pour on the cider vinegar, and set aside to marinate.

2 Place the fish in a large shallow pan and add sufficient court bouillon to just cover them. Slowly bring to the boil, then immediately lower the heat until the liquid is barely moving. Poach the fish for about 10 minutes, until the flesh is no longer pink inside. Carefully lift out the fish onto warmed plates; keep warm.

3 Drain the onion and set aside, reserving the vinegar.

4 Dry-fry the mustard seeds in a heavy-based skillet over a high heat until they begin to pop. Immediately add the butter, and, as soon as it melts, add the vinegar.

5 Pour the sizzling butter over the fish and scatter with the red onion and parsley. Garnish with caper berries or capers, and serve at once.

Note To make a court bouillon, put 7 cups water in a large pan with
½ red onion, sliced, 6 peppercorns, 2 teaspoons salt, 6 mustard seeds, and
1 tablespoon cider vinegar. Bring to the boil, lower the heat, and simmer
for 5 minutes.

Skate wings have a delicate texture and a fine flavor. For optimum results, soak the skate in salted water in the fridge before poaching. You can substitute flounder or catfish.

Smoked salmon and leek risotto

5 tablespoons olive oil

1 pound medium leeks, thinly sliced

2 garlic cloves, finely chopped

1 pound 2 ounces arborio or other risotto rice

1¼ cups medium white wine

5 cups well flavored fish stock (approximately)

⅓ pound sliced smoked salmon, roughly chopped

salt and pepper

To serve

crème fraîche

lumpfish roe or salmon caviar (optional)

1 Heat the olive oil in a heavy-based pan. Add the leeks, and sauté for a few minutes until lightly colored and beginning to soften. Stir in the garlic and cook for 2–3 minutes.

2 Add the rice and stir well to coat with oil. Add the wine and boil until totally reduced.

3 Meanwhile, bring the stock to a simmer in another pan.

4 Add a large ladleful of stock to the rice, and stir until it is absorbed. Continue to add the stock in this way, making sure that each addition is absorbed before adding more, until the rice is tender and creamy, but firm to the bite.

5 Gently fold in the smoked salmon. Season generously with pepper and salt to taste. Cover and leave to rest for 1 minute. Serve topped with crème fraîche, and lumpfish roe or salmon caviar if wished.

A luxurious risotto flavored with wine, sautéed leeks, and lots of smoked salmon. For a special supper, top with a spoonful of crème fraîche and a little lumpfish roe or salmon caviar.

Mediterranean fish stew

Illustrated on previous pages

4 tablespoons olive oil
1 onion, minced
5 garlic cloves, minced
1 small fennel bulb, minced
3 celery sticks, minced
15-ounce can chopped tomatoes
1 tablespoon fresh thyme leaves
1 bay leaf
grated rind and juice of ½ orange
2-inch strip of lemon peel

1 teaspoon saffron strands
3 cups fresh fish stock (see note)
3 tablespoons Pernod
9 ounces thick cod fillet
9 ounces sea bass or hoki fillet
9 ounces raw tiger shrimp, shelled
   and deveined
3 tablespoons finely chopped fresh
   flat leaf parsley
salt and pepper

1 Heat the oil in a large saucepan. Add the onion, garlic, fennel, and celery, and cook on a low heat, stirring occasionally, for 15–20 minutes until the vegetables are soft and just starting to color.
2 Add the tomatoes with their juice, thyme, bay leaf, orange rind and juice, lemon peel and saffron. Cook briskly for 5 minutes, then add fish stock and Pernod, and bring to the boil. Turn the heat down and simmer for 20 minutes.
3 Meanwhile, cut the cod and sea bass into 2-inch cubes. Add to the pan and cook for 3 minutes, then add shrimp and cook for another 3 minutes.
4 Stir in the chopped parsley, and check the seasoning. Serve in warmed bowls with hot bread to mop up the delicious juices. Accompany with salad.

Note To make your own stock, ask your fish dealer for the fish bones and trimmings. Put in a pan with the shrimp shells, 2–3 onion slices, a handful of parsley sprigs, a bay leaf, and a few peppercorns. Add water to cover, bring to the boil, and simmer for 20 minutes. Strain and use as required.

This version of the famous Mediterranean fish stew features cod, sea bass, and tiger shrimp.

Chinese-style sea bass

1 bunch green onions, finely
  shredded
2 sea bass, each about 1½ pound,
  cleaned
1⅛ teaspoon Chinese five-spice
  powder
1½-inch piece fresh gingerroot,
  shredded

3 garlic cloves, finely sliced
½ teaspoon black or toasted white
  sesame seeds
3 tablespoons sunflower oil
5 tablespoons light soy sauce

1 Preheat oven to 450°F. Put the shredded green onion in a bowl, add some
cold water to cover, and chill in the fridge to curl the onion shreds.

2 Make deep slashes in both sides of the fish, about 1 inch apart. Rub the
spice powder into the cuts and inside the cavity. Place the sea bass on a large
heatproof serving plate.

3 Drain the green onion; pat dry. Scatter the onion, ginger, garlic, and
sesame seeds over the fish. Place some scrunched-up balls of foil over the
base of a large roasting pan, and carefully position the plate of fish on top.
Pour the oil and soy sauce over.

4 Pour a 1½-inch depth of boiling water into the roasting pan, then cover
with foil to form a tent over the fish; secure the foil under the edge of the
pan to hold in the steam during baking.

5 Carefully place in the oven, and bake for about 12–16 minutes, depending
on size, until the sea bass is tender. Serve with rice and stir-fried vegetables.

Note The fish is cooked when the flesh divides into flakes easily.

An impressive steamed fish to bring to
the table whole. Serve with plain rice and
a colorful medley of stir-fried vegetables.

Monkfish skewers

4 monkfish fillets, each 7 ounces,
  skinned
juice of 1 small lemon
1 teaspoon fennel seeds
salt and pepper

4 shallots (unpeeled)
1 red bell pepper, cored, seeded and
  cut into 12 pieces
a little olive oil, for brushing
lemon wedges, to serve

1 Cut each monkfish fillet into 5 or 6 pieces, and place in a bowl with
the lemon juice, fennel seeds, salt, and pepper; toss to mix, and set aside.
2 Put the shallots in a pan, cover with cold water, and bring to the boil.
Simmer gently for 6–8 minutes. then drain and refresh in cold water. Peel
and quarter the shallots lengthwise.
3 Preheat the broiler to medium. Thread the monkfish chunks onto 4 long
skewers, alternating with the red pepper and shallots.
4 Brush with a little olive oil, and grill for 12–15 minutes, turning the
skewers occasionally. Serve with lemon wedges, a leafy salad, and warm bread.

Firm-fleshed monkfish is the perfect choice
to thread onto skewers, though prime cod
fillet could substitute. Ask the fish dealer to
fillet and skin the fish for you.

Greek baked mackerel plaki

4 large mackerel, cleaned
  and trimmed
salt and pepper
juice of 2 lemons
3 garlic cloves, minced
1 teaspoon fresh thyme leaves

4 plum tomatoes, skinned, seeded,
  and diced
20 black olives, stoned and chopped
4 tablespoons olive oil
5 tablespoons dry white wine

1 Cut 3 slashes on both sides of each fish, and place in an oiled large, shallow ovenproof dish; season well. Pour the lemon juice over, cover, and leave to marinate in a cool place for 1 hour, turning occasionally.
2 Preheat oven to 375°F. Spoon the remaining ingredients over the fish. Bake for 15–20 minutes, until cooked.
3 Serve with rice and a green salad, topped with crumbled feta and thin red onion slices.

Fresh mackerel baked with lemon, garlic, thyme, black olives, and white wine—to delicious effect.

Moroccan grilled cod

4 cod fillets, each 6–7 ounces,
  skinned
For the chermoula
2 tablespoons roughly chopped fresh
  cilantro
1 tablespoon chopped fresh mint
1 tablespoon chopped flat leaf
  parsley

2 garlic cloves, chopped
1 red chile, seeded and chopped
1 teaspoon paprika
1½ teaspoon roasted cumin seeds
1 teaspoon saffron strands
5 tablespoons olive oil
juice of 1 lemon
1½ teaspoon salt

1 Place the fish fillets in a shallow ceramic or glass dish.
2 Put the chermoula ingredients in a food processor and blend until smooth.
Spoon over the fish and turn to coat. Cover and marinate in the fridge for
at least 2 hours, ideally overnight, turning occasionally.
3 Preheat broiler to medium-high. Lift the fish out of the marinade and grill
for 5–7 minutes on each side or until lightly browned and cooked through.
Check the seasoning. Serve with warm pita bread and yogurt.

Chermoula, a Moroccan spice and herb mix,
transforms cod into an exciting dish.

Seared tuna with fennel and thyme

4 tuna or swordfish steaks, each
  7 ounces
salt and pepper
3 tablespoons Pernod
2 tablespoons olive oil
zest and juice of 1 lemon
2 teaspoons fresh thyme leaves
2 teaspoons fennel seeds, lightly
  roasted
4 sun-dried tomatoes, finely chopped
1 teaspoons dried chile flakes

For the salsa
4 plum tomatoes, skinned, seeded,
  and sliced
2 tablespoons shredded fresh basil
  leaves
1 red chile, seeded and finely sliced
3 tablespoons extra virgin olive oil
2 teaspoons balsamic vinegar
1 teaspoon superfine sugar
For the garnish
thyme sprigs

1 Season the fish and place in a shallow dish. In a bowl, mix together
the Pernod, olive oil, lemon zest and juice, thyme, fennel seeds, sun-dried
tomatoes, and chile. Pour over the fish, cover, and leave to marinate
in a cool place for 1–2 hours.
2 Meanwhile, combine the ingredients for the salsa in a bowl. Season,
then cover and set aside to allow the flavors to infuse.
3 To cook the fish, preheat a lightly oiled grill pan or a heavy-based skillet
over a high heat. When very hot, cook the fish steaks for 3–4 minutes
on each side; they should still be a little pink in the middle.
4 Transfer the fish steaks to warmed plates, garnish, and serve with the salsa.

Hearty fresh tuna or swordfish steaks are
marinated with Mediterranean flavors, then
quickly seared on a hot grill pan. A tomato
and basil salsa is the ideal complement.

Salmon on lemon pasta salad with salsa

4 small skinless salmon fillets, each about 5 ounces (see note)
½ pound dried fusilli or other pasta shapes
5 tablespoons extra-virgin olive oil
2 teaspoons fresh thyme leaves
1 tablespoon lemon juice
1 tablespoon black peppercorns, crushed
1 teaspoon cumin seeds

For the salsa
¼ teaspoon saffron strands
3 tomatoes, peeled, seeded, and diced
3 green onions, minced
1 garlic clove, crushed
1 tablespoon shredded fresh basil
salt and pepper
For the garnish
basil leaves

1 First make the salsa. Soak the saffron in 1 tablespoon boiling water for 10 minutes, then mix with the other salsa ingredients; set aside.
2 Cook the pasta in boiling salted water until al dente.
3 Meanwhile, in a small pan, warm 4 tablespoons of the oil with the thyme, lemon juice, and seasoning. Drain the pasta thoroughly and toss with the dressing. Leave to cool.
4 Preheat a grill pan or heavy-based skillet until very hot. Combine the peppercorns and cumin seeds, and press firmly onto the salmon fillets. Brush with the remaining oil.
5 Add the salmon to the grill pan and sear for 1½ minutes each side. Remove from the pan, let cool slightly, then slice thickly.
6 Arrange the pasta salad on plates, and top with the warm salmon slices. Spoon around the saffron salsa and serve garnished with basil leaves.

Note Make sure that you use the freshest possible salmon for this dish.

Salmon is seared quickly over a high heat, so the outside is crisp and slightly charred, while the center remains rare and moist.

Broiled cod with ham and gruyère

4 thick skinless cod fillets, each
   about 7 ounces
salt and pepper
¾ cup pitted green olives, sliced
¼ pound gruyère cheese, finely
   grated
2 ounces wafer-thin smoked ham

1 Preheat the broiler. Lay the fish fillets in an ovenproof dish, season,
then broil for 2–3 minutes. Mix the olives and cheese together.
2 Turn the fish steaks over and top with the ham. Scatter with the cheese
and olives.
3 Broil for another 4–5 minutes until the cheese is golden and bubbling
and the fish fillets are cooked through to the middle. Serve with a salad
and crusty bread.

Succulent cod fillets are complemented here
by the rich flavors and colors of smoked ham,
gruyère cheese, and olives.

Saltimbocca of sole

2 sole, filleted and skinned
8 slices of Parma ham
16 basil leaves
pepper
4 tablespoons unsalted butter
⅝ cup chicken stock

⅝ cup heavy cream
4 tablespoons white wine
1 teaspoon Dijon mustard
1 tablespoon finely chopped fresh
    flat leaf parsley

1 Preheat oven to 400°F. Trim the sole fillets, then cut each in half lengthwise.
2 Lay the slices of Parma ham on a board, place 2 basil leaves on each, and cover with a sole fillet. Season with pepper. Starting from the tail end, roll up fairly tightly, making sure the fish is covered by the ham. Repeat to make the remaining rolls.
3 Melt 2 tablespoons of the butter in a large skillet. When sizzling, carefully add the fish rolls, seam side down, and cook for 1–2 minutes on each side, until golden brown.
4 Carefully place the rolls, seam side down, on a baking tray lined with waxed paper, and bake for 8–10 minutes.
5 Meanwhile, make the sauce. Put the stock, cream, wine, and mustard in a small pan, and bring to the boil, stirring. Simmer for 4–5 minutes until reduced and slightly thickened, then whisk in the remaining butter. Season with pepper to taste, and add the parsley.
6 To serve, spoon the sauce onto 4 warmed plates, and arrange 2 saltimboccas on each plate. Serve at once, with fluffy mashed potatoes and wilted collard greens.

Sole fillets are wrapped in Parma ham and served with a delicious mild creamy mustard sauce.

Salmon with ginger and cilantro

Illustrated on previous pages

Serves 3–4; or 8 as a starter

1 pound 2 ounces salmon fillet (tail end), with skin

1-inch piece fresh gingerroot, peeled

3 handfuls fresh cilantro leaves, chopped

1 teaspoon coriander seeds

1 tablespoon coarse salt

1 tablespoon superfine sugar

freshly ground black pepper

1 Trim the salmon, removing any bones.

2 Coarsely chop the ginger, and squeeze out the juice onto the salmon, using a garlic press. Mix remaining ingredients together, and press onto both sides of the fish.

3 Lay the fish, skin side down, in a shallow dish large enough to hold it flat. Cover with baking parchment, place a board on top, and weight down. Leave to marinate in the fridge for 3–4 days, turning fish each day.

4 Blot excess oil from fish with paper towels. Slice thinly, on the diagonal, avoiding skin. Serve with arugula and rye bread.

Very fresh salmon is essential for this raw marinated dish.

Italian seafood risotto

3 tablespoons extra-virgin olive oil

3 garlic cloves, minced

7 ounces salmon fillet, skinned and cut into 1-inch cubes

9 ounces raw tiger shrimp, shelled and deveined

4 baby squid, cleaned and cut into rings

½ cup dry white wine

6 cups fish stock

3 tablespoons butter

4 shallots, minced

½ red pepper, cored, seeded, and diced

1 plum tomato, skinned, seeded and chopped

2 cups arborio rice

salt and pepper

2 tablespoons finely chopped fresh flat leaf parsley

1 Heat 2 tablespoons of the oil in a large saucepan, add the garlic and sauté for 1 minute. Add the salmon, shrimp and squid, and stir-fry for 3 minutes, then add the wine and bring to a simmer. Remove the fish and shellfish with a slotted spoon and set aside.

2 Add the fish stock to the pan; set aside.

3 Melt 2 tablespoons of the butter in another large pan with the remaining oil. Add the shallots and cook until golden. Add the red pepper, tomato, and rice; cook, stirring, for 2 minutes.

4 Meanwhile, bring the stock to a simmer. Gradually stir the stock into the rice mixture, about ⅛ cup at a time, ensuring that each addition is absorbed before adding more. Continue until the rice is tender. With the last addition of stock, add the seafood and season to taste.

5 Stir in the remaining butter and chopped parsley. Serve at once.

Note The cooking time is about 20 minutes, from the first addition of the stock. Depending on the variety of rice, you may need to use a little less or more liquid.

A creamy, wine-enriched risotto, liberally flavored with fresh salmon, tiger shrimp and baby squid.

chicken

Chargrilled chicken stacks with basil

Serves 4

4 free-range chicken breast fillets, skinned
1 large red bell pepper
1 large yellow bell pepper
2 medium-small eggplants
salt and pepper
5 tablespoons extra-virgin olive oil

For the basil dressing

16 fresh basil leaves, roughly torn
2 tablespoons cider vinegar
6 tablespoons olive oil
½ teaspoon Dijon mustard

For the garnish

basil leaves

1 Using a sharp knife, slice each chicken breast into 3 even medallions.

2 Cut off the tops and a little of the base from the peppers, then cut each one into four, to give even, flat pieces; discard seeds. Cut the eggplants into 12 even slices, about ¼ inch thick.

3 Put the chicken and vegetables in a large shallow dish, season and pour the oil over. Mix well, cover, and leave to marinate in a cool place for at least 30 minutes (or up to 3 hours).

4 Put the dressing ingredients in a blender, season, and pulse until amalgamated but retaining some flecks of basil.

5 Preheat a grill pan (or broiler) to high. Sear the chicken and vegetables in batches to obtain a charred effect on both sides; turn down the heat to cook right through.

6 To assemble, halve the pepper pieces. Place a chicken medallion on each plate, and stack the vegetables and remaining chicken medallions on top, alternating the colors and finishing with yellow pepper. Serve hot or cold, drizzled with the dressing and garnished with basil leaves.

Note The stacks can be assembled ahead in a deep dish, covered and warmed through in the oven to serve.

Serve these chicken stacks with flavored breads and a leafy salad.

Eggplant and chicken roulades

Illustrated on previous pages

1 pound skinless chicken breast fillets, or skinned boneless thighs, or a mixture

1 rounded tablespoon half-fat crème fraîche

2 tablespoons finely shredded fresh basil

salt and pepper

2 medium-large eggplants

oil, for brushing

For the tomato sauce

2 teaspoons olive oil

1 small onion or 2 shallots, finely chopped

1 garlic clove, crushed

2¼ cups passata

few basil leaves

1 tablespoon red or white wine

1 Mince the chicken meat or finely chop in a food processor; transfer to a bowl. Mix in the crème fraîche, basil, salt, and pepper.

2 Thinly slice the eggplants lengthwise, to give 10–12 slices from each; discard the outer, skin-covered slices. Brush one side of each eggplant slice with a little oil, and place, oiled-side down, on a work surface.

3 Divide the chicken mixture between the eggplant slices, and spread evenly, almost to the edges. Roll up the eggplant slices to enclose the filling and thread onto 4 wooden kabob skewers. Place on a nonstick baking sheet. Preheat oven to 375°F.

4 To make the sauce, heat the oil in a pan and fry the onion for 3–4 minutes until softened, then add the garlic and cook for 1 minute. Add the passata, basil leaves, and wine. Bring to the boil, reduce the heat, and simmer gently for about 10 minutes. Season to taste.

5 Meanwhile, cook the eggplant rolls in the oven for about 20–25 minutes, until the chicken is cooked through, turning halfway through the cooking time. Serve with the tomato sauce and a leafy green salad.

Oven-baked eggplant slices rolled around a tasty minced chicken filling.

Pan-fried chicken with shiitake

2 tablespoons unsalted butter
4 chicken breast fillets (with skin)
2 garlic cloves, finely chopped
5 ounces small shiitake mushrooms
4 tablespoons extra-dry white
vermouth

1¼ cups fresh chicken stock
4 tablespoons crème fraîche
salt and pepper
4 green onions, shredded

1 Melt the butter in a large skillet. Add the chicken, and cook gently for 5 minutes, turning once. Remove and set aside.

2 Add the garlic and mushrooms to the pan; stir-fry until the mushrooms start to soften.

3 Add the vermouth and stock. Increase heat and boil rapidly until the liquid has almost totally evaporated.

4 Stir in the crème fraîche, season, then return the chicken to the pan. Part cover and simmer for 5 minutes or until the chicken is cooked through. Stir in the onions and heat through. Serve with tagliatelle.

Pan-fried chicken readily takes on flavors and cooks quickly, so it's perfect for a fast midweek supper.

Golden tapenade chicken breasts

Illustrated on previous pages

4 boned chicken breasts with skin
    and wing bone attached (see note)
3 ounces ricotta cheese
4 tablespoons black olive tapenade

4 sun-dried tomatoes in oil, chopped
salt and pepper
olive oil, for brushing

1 Preheat oven to 400°F. Break up the ricotta in a bowl, then beat in the tapenade, sun-dried tomatoes, and salt and pepper to taste.
2 Loosen the skin covering each chicken breast, and push in as much stuffing as will fit between the skin and the flesh. Gently re-form the skin over the stuffing and chicken.
3 Brush the skin with olive oil, and season well. Place in a baking dish and bake in the oven for 25 minutes.
4 Allow the chicken to rest for 5 minutes before serving, with roasted peppers and new potatoes or rice.

Note If your supermarket does not have chicken breasts prepared in this way, ask a butcher to prepare them specially for you.

Variation Add a spoonful of chopped capers to the stuffing to cut the richness and add a delicious piquancy.

Cut into these moist chicken breasts to reveal a soft, savory stuffing—reminiscent of the flavors of Provence.

Coq au vin with thyme and juniper

2–3 tablespoons olive oil

8 slices smoked bacon, halved crosswise and rolled up

9 ounces shallots, peeled (see note)

9 ounces baby button mushrooms

8 boneless chicken thighs, skinned

2 tablespoons seasoned flour

1¼ cup Beaujolais

2 tablespoons brandy

1¼ cup chicken stock

1 tablespoon tomato purée

2 garlic cloves, chopped

4 juniper berries, crushed

1 tablespoon fresh thyme leaves

salt and pepper

1 Preheat oven to 350°F. Heat 2 tablespoons olive oil in a large heavy-based skillet, and fry the bacon rolls for a few minutes until turning golden; transfer to a flameproof casserole, using a slotted spoon.

2 Fry the shallots and mushrooms in the oil left in the pan for a few minutes, turning, until slightly colored. Add to the casserole.

3 Coat the chicken thighs in the seasoned flour, then fry for about 5 minutes until golden, adding more oil to the pan if necessary. Transfer to the casserole.

4 Pour the wine, brandy, and stock into the pan. Stir in the tomato paste, garlic, juniper and thyme. Bring to the boil, then pour over the chicken.

5 Cover tightly and cook the casserole in the oven for 1 hour or until the chicken and shallots are tender; check the seasoning. If preparing ahead, cool and refrigerate for up to 3 days.

6 When ready to serve, reheat on the cooktop until bubbling. Serve with green beans and sautéed potatoes.

Note Before peeling shallots, immerse in boiling water for 5 minutes—you will find the skins come away much more easily.

Juniper berries add an intriguing and subtle fragrance to this version of a classic, which is ideal for entertaining.

Pan-seared chicken with garlic sauce

4 tablespoons butter
4 boneless chicken breasts
  (with skin)
12 garlic cloves, unpeeled

1¼ cup dry or medium white wine
2 large fresh rosemary sprigs
2 fresh bay leaves
salt and pepper

1 Melt the butter in a sauté pan. When foaming, add the chicken, skin-side down and the unpeeled garlic cloves. Fry for about 5 minutes, then turn the chicken over.

2 Add the wine and herbs. Season, then cover tightly and simmer for 20 minutes. Transfer the chicken to a warmed plate, and leave to rest in a warm place.

3 Mash most of the garlic into the sauce, using a potato masher, then bring to the boil, taste, and season. Strain the sauce over the chicken, or pour it over—bits and all! Serve with sugar-snap or snow peas and new potatoes.

A real must for garlic lovers—whole cloves are cooked with chicken fillets, then mashed into the sauce.

Tandoori chicken pieces

Illustrated on previous pages

8–12 skinless chicken pieces (thighs, drumsticks, halved breasts)
juice of 1 lemon
sea salt
For the marinade
generous 1 cup yogurt
1 onion, cut into chunks
3 garlic cloves, crushed

1-inch piece fresh gingerroot, chopped
2 tablespoons turmeric
1 green chilli, seeded
1 tablespoon garam masala
To serve
lime wedges

1 Cut deep slits in the meatiest parts of the chicken pieces, and place in a shallow dish. Sprinkle with lemon juice and salt and let stand for 30 minutes.
2 Meanwhile, blend all the marinade ingredients together in a food processor or blender to form a smooth paste. Add the chicken pieces and toss to coat. Cover and leave to marinate in a cool place for several hours, or overnight if possible.
3 Preheat a baking sheet in the oven at 500°F. Lift the chicken out of the marinade and place the drumsticks and thighs on the hot baking sheet. Bake for about 20 minutes, adding the chicken breast pieces after about 5 minutes.
4 Serve with lime wedges and warm naan bread or rice.

Note An Indian-style salad of tomato, cucumber, and chopped onion, scattered with plenty of chopped fresh cilantro is the ideal accompaniment.

For optimum flavor, slash the chicken pieces and then leave to marinate in the tandoori mixture overnight.

Basil-wrapped chicken and mushroom stuffing

4 chicken breast fillets, with skin

For the stuffing

½ cup dried porcini (or other dried mushrooms)

1 tablespoon olive oil

1 small garlic clove, crushed

1 shallot, minced

½ cup minced mushrooms

2 ounces creamy, soft goat cheese

2 tablespoons chopped fresh parsley

salt and pepper

4 tablespoons unsalted butter, softened

12 large basil leaves

squeeze of lemon juice

scant ½ cup dry white wine

1 Preheat the oven to 400°F. Put the dried mushrooms into a small bowl, pour on just enough warm water to cover, and set aside to soak for 15 minutes.

2 Meanwhile, loosen the skin from one side of each chicken breast, working your fingers under the skin, keeping it attached on the opposite side.

3 Drain the porcini, reserving the soaking liquid, and chop finely. Heat the olive oil in a heavy-based skillet, add the garlic and shallot, and cook gently for 5 minutes or until softened. Add the fresh and dried mushrooms, and cook until softened and almost dry. Take off the heat and cool slightly.

4 Add the goat cheese and parsley to the stuffing, and season well with salt and pepper. Mix until evenly combined, then leave to cool completely.

5 When the stuffing is cold, carefully spoon it under the chicken breast skin with a teaspoon, and spread evenly. Push a fine wooden skewer through the skin and breast along the open side to secure. Put the chicken breasts, skin-side uppermost and side by side, in a small roasting pan.

6 Smear the softened butter on top of the skin, and lay the basil leaves on top. Season with salt and pepper, and sprinkle with the lemon juice. Pour the reserved mushroom soaking liquid into the tin, leaving behind the sediment, then add wine. Bake for 25 minutes, or until the chicken is cooked through.

7 Serve the chicken breasts drizzled with the pan juices and accompanied by zucchini and new potatoes or rice.

Note Choose chicken breasts that are generously covered with skin that is intact, to hold the stuffing in place.

Chicken with caramelized apples

Serves 6

6 corn-fed chicken breast fillets
   (with skin)
salt and pepper
4 tablespoons unsalted butter
⅝ cup heavy cream

3 large, flavorful eating apples,
   about 1 pound in total
2 tablespoons sunflower oil
14 ounces shallots, peeled
3 tablespoons calvados or brandy

1 Preheat oven to 375°F. Season the chicken with salt and pepper.
2 Melt half the butter in a flameproof casserole. Add the chicken, skin side down, and fry for about 3 minutes until golden brown. Turn and brown the other side.
3 Add half the cream, cover, and cook in the oven for 20–25 minutes.
4 Meanwhile quarter, core, and slice the apples. Heat the oil in a large heavy-based skillet and fry the shallots for 8 minutes until browned. Add remaining butter, and fry the apples for about 5 minutes, turning, until evenly golden; keep warm.
5 Remove casserole from oven and place on a high heat. Pour in the remaining cream and let bubble for 1 minute. Add half the apples and shallots. Add the calvados, cover, and turn off the heat.
6 Pile the remaining shallots and apples on top of the chicken, and drizzle with the sauce to serve.

A delicious brew of rich flavors just begging to be piled onto a mound of mashed celeriac and potatoes.

Bronzed paprika chicken

Illustrated on previous pages

Serves 4–6

1 oven-ready chicken, about
  3½ pounds
salt and pepper
1 unwaxed lemon, halved
small sprig of fresh bay leaves
4 tablespoons butter, softened
4 teaspoons paprika

¼ tsp cayenne pepper
2–3 whole garlic bulbs, halved
  crosswise
1 tablespoon olive oil
1 pound cherry tomatoes on the vine
2½ ounces finely sliced chorizo
  sausage
bay leaves, to garnish

1 Remove any excess fat from the cavity of the chicken, and season. Place the lemon halves and bay leaves inside.

2 Loosen the skin away from the chicken breast and legs, then smear the butter onto the flesh under the skin to keep it moist. Mix the paprika, ¼ teaspoon salt, ¼ teaspoon pepper, and the cayenne; rub all over the skin. Tie the legs together and put the chicken on a trivet in a large roasting pan

3 Preheat oven to 375°F, and estimate cooking time, 20 minutes per pound, plus 20 minutes. Place chicken in a roasting pan. Toss garlic in olive oil and place around the bird. Roast in oven; baste occasionally.

4 About 10 minutes before end of the roasting time, toss the tomatoes in the remaining olive oil and add to the roasting pan.

5 Ensure chicken is cooked by piercing the thickest part of the leg with a skewer: the juices should be clear and golden; if pink, roast for a little longer.

6 Transfer to a warmed platter, and let rest for 10–15 minutes. Meanwhile, fry the chorizo slices in a dry pan over a high heat until crisp. Scatter on the chicken, and surround with tomatoes and garlic. Garnish with bay leaves.

You can prepare the chicken for roasting a few hours ahead. Keep in the refrigerator, but bring to room temperature before cooking.

Maple roast poussins with thyme

4 poussins (baby chicken)
6 tablespoons maple syrup
1 tablespoon Dijon mustard
3 garlic cloves, crushed

1½ teaspoon fresh lemon thyme
 leaves
salt and pepper

1 Preheat oven to 425°F. Halve the poussins lengthwise along the breast bone, using poultry shears or kitchen scissors, and remove the tips from the wings and knuckles. Place in a large dish.
2 Mix together the maple syrup, mustard, garlic, lemon thyme, and seasoning until well blended. Spoon over the poussins and turn them in the mixture to coat all over.
3 Arrange the poussins, close together, in a large roasting dish, and spoon the remaining juices over. Then roast for 25–30 minutes until golden. Serve with vegetables.

Less sweet than honey, maple syrup marries with the citrus fragrance of lemon thyme to add succulence and flavor to poussins.

Spicy chicken cakes

Illustrated on previous pages

Serves 3–4

¾ pound ground chicken

2 tablespoons Thai red curry paste

1 medium egg, beaten

2 tablespoons cornstarch

2 kaffir lime leaves (see note), finely
  shredded

2 tablespoons chopped fresh cilantro

2 green onions, finely sliced

1 red chile, seeded and finely sliced

oil for deep-frying

1 Put the ground chicken, red curry paste and about half of the egg in
a food processor; process until evenly blended. Transfer to a mixing bowl.
2 Add the cornstarch, lime leaves, cilantro, green onions, and chile. Mix
well, using your fingers, adding more egg, if necessary, to bind the mixture.
3 Divide the mixture into 12 portions, and roll each into a ball. Mold and
flatten each ball into a "cake" about 2 inches in diameter and ¼ inch thick.
4 Heat a 2-inch depth of oil in a wok or sauté pan. Deep-fry the cakes, a
few at a time, for about 5 minutes, until lightly browned and cooked.
5 Drain on crumpled paper towels, and serve hot with a salsa, as an
appetizer or with a salad as a starter or light lunch.

Note Kaffir lime leaves are available in packs of mixed Thai flavorings from
some supermarkets. If unobtainable, use the grated zest of 2 limes.

These tasty morsels are great as an appetizer
with drinks. Serve with a fresh tomato,
cucumber, cilantro, and red onion salsa—
spiked with lime juice.

Tuscan chicken thighs

4–6 garlic cloves, peeled
2 teaspoons sea salt
1 teaspoon freshly ground black
   pepper
3 tablespoons finely chopped fresh
   rosemary

12 boneless chicken thighs, skinned
12 thin slices pancetta or streaky
   bacon
12 fresh bay leaves
olive oil, for brushing

1 Pound the garlic with the salt, pepper, and rosemary, using a pestle and mortar or coffee grinder. Rub this paste generously all over the flesh side of the chicken thighs.

2 Reshape and wrap each thigh in a slice of pancetta, tucking in a bay leaf. Secure with fine string. Preheat the broiler.

3 Place the chicken in the broiler pan and brush with olive oil. Broil for 15–20 minutes, turning every 5 minutes until golden, crisp, and cooked through. Serve drizzled with extra olive oil and accompanied by a salad.

Rosemary, garlic, and plenty of seasoning give these succulent chicken thighs an authentic Tuscan flavour.

Spicy chicken korma with cashews

2 onions, quartered
4 garlic cloves
3-inch piece fresh gingerroot, chopped
1 cup cashew nuts
3 tablespoons sunflower oil
2 red chiles, seeded and sliced
1 teaspoon cumin seeds
1 teaspoon ground turmeric
1 teaspoon ground white pepper
3 cups chicken stock
4 skinless chicken breast fillets, cubed
⅝ cup yogurt
2 bananas, sliced
3 tablespoons chopped fresh cilantro
cilantro sprigs, to garnish

1 Put the onions, garlic, ginger, and nuts in a food processor, and blend to a paste.
2 Heat the oil in a large skillet, add the onion and cashew mixture with the chile and cumin, and fry for 10 minutes, stirring frequently.
3 Stir in the turmeric and pepper, then pour in the stock and simmer for 5 minutes.
4 Add the chicken, cover and simmer gently for 15 minutes.
5 Stir in the yogurt, bananas, and cilantro. Garnish with sprigs of cilantro, and serve with basmati rice or naan bread.

Fresh ginger and chiles impart flavor, while ground cashew nuts give this curry an intriguing texture.

Pancetta-wrapped roast chicken

1 oven-ready chicken, about
   3¼ pounds
7 ounces Italian-style sausages,
   skinned
7 ounces cooked chestnuts
   (preferably roasted), roughly
   chopped

salt and pepper
10 thin slices pancetta
oil, for brushing

1 Preheat oven to 400°F. Break up the sausage meat with a fork, and mix
with the chestnuts and plenty of pepper. Use to stuff the neck end of the
chicken (not the cavity). Secure the flap under the bird with a toothpick.
2 Season the chicken with plenty of pepper, then lay the pancetta slices,
overlapping slightly, over the surface of the chicken.
3 Put the chicken on a trivet in a roasting dish. Cover with a piece of oiled
baking parchment, securing at each "corner" of the chicken with a
toothpick. Roast for 50 minutes, then carefully remove the paper. Roast for
another 30–40 minutes until the chicken is cooked.

Notes To calculate roasting time, weigh the chicken and allow 20 minutes
per pound, plus an extra 20 minutes at 375°F. To test that a roast chicken
is cooked, pierce the thickest part of the leg with a skewer and make sure
that the juices run clear.

Tasty chicken with an Italian stuffing, roasted
in a crisp pancetta overcoat.

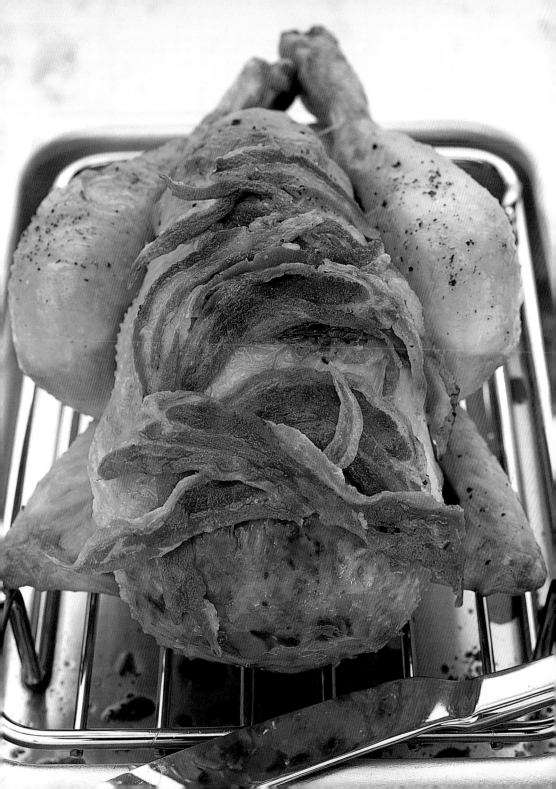

Thai broiled chicken with cilantro

Illustrated on previous pages

4 corn-fed chicken breasts (with skin)
2 garlic cloves, chopped
¼ pound fresh coriander leaves, chopped
2 handfuls fresh mint leaves, chopped
2 teaspoons ground cumin
2 teaspoons ground coriander

1 red chile, sliced
juice and grated rind of 1 lime
2 teaspoons soft brown sugar
1 cup coconut milk
2 teaspoons coarse salt
arugula leaves, to garnish
lime wedges, to serve

1 Lay the chicken breasts, skin side up, on a board. With a sharp knife, make 3–4 shallow cuts in each one. Place the chicken breasts in a shallow dish, in which they fit snugly.

2 Put all the remaining ingredients into a food processor, and blend until fairly smooth. Pour this marinade over the chicken, and turn each piece to coat thoroughly. Cover and leave to marinate for at least 1 hour.

3 Preheat the broiler to high. Remove the chicken from the marinade, and place, skin side up, on a lightly oiled broiler pan. Broil for 8–10 minutes or until browned, then turn, baste with the marinade, and broil the other side for 6–8 minutes or until cooked through.

4 Serve hot, garnished with arugula leaves and accompanied by lime wedges, steamed Thai fragrant rice flavored with cilantro, and a green salad.

Broiled to a crust, these fragrant chicken portions are deliciously moist within.

Thai-style risotto

2 tablespoons sunflower oil
6 green onions, finely sliced
1 lemongrass stalk, finely sliced
1 teaspoon crushed garlic
1 teaspoon finely grated fresh
  gingerroot
1¾ cup arborio (risotto) rice
10 ounces chicken breast, cut into
  ¾-inch cubes

¼ pound shiitake mushrooms, sliced
5 cups good-quality chicken stock
  (see note)
4 tablespoons chopped fresh cilantro
salt and pepper
shredded green onion, to garnish

1 Heat the oil in a large heavy-based saucepan. Add the green onions, lemongrass, garlic, and ginger and stir-fry for 1 minute.
2 Add the rice; cook, stirring, for a few minutes, then add the chicken and mushrooms. Stir-fry for another 2–3 minutes.
3 Add a ladleful of the stock, and cook gently, stirring frequently, until it is absorbed. Continue adding the stock, a ladleful at a time as each addition is absorbed, until the rice is creamy in texture.
4 Add the remaining stock and cilantro. Season well, and stir over a low heat for a few minutes longer or until the rice is just tender and moist.
5 Serve immediately, garnished with shredded green onion.

Note Use homemade stock, or buy fresh chicken stock from a supermarket or delicatessen.

Subtle Eastern flavors give this Italian classic an original Thai twist.

Saffron roast chicken

1 oven-ready chicken, about
  3½ pounds
For the saffron butter
4 tablespoons unsalted butter,
  softened
2 large pinches of saffron threads,
  crumbled
½ teaspoon salt
For the onions
1 tablespoon olive oil

2 tablespoons butter
1 pound onions, halved and
  thinly sliced
2 teaspoons garam masala
2 teaspoons cumin seeds
6 cardamom pods, lightly crushed
2 teaspoons finely chopped fresh
  gingerroot
generous ¼ cup golden raisins

1 Preheat oven to 400°F. Loosen the skin from the chicken breast by easing your fingers under the neck flap, over the breast and down to the legs, without puncturing the skin.

2 Mix the ingredients for the saffron butter, and spread evenly over the chicken breast under the skin. Secure the neck flap under the bird with a toothpick.

3 Heat the oil and butter in a wide pan, and gently fry the onions until softened. Add all the spices, and cook for 2–3 minutes. Add the raisins, then transfer to a roasting dish and place the chicken on top, breast side down. Roast for 45 minutes.

4 Lower setting to 375°F, and turn the chicken breast side up. Stir the onions, piling some of the lighter ones on top of the chicken to keep it moist. Roast for another 45 minutes or until the chicken is cooked through and the onions are crisp.

Note Roasting the chicken breast-side down to start with helps to keep the breast meat succulent and moist.

Saffron butter-basted chicken roasted on a bed of sliced onion flavored with spices.

Steamed Thai chicken parcels

Illustrated on previous pages

4 large banana leaves (see note)
1 tablespoon vegetable oil
4 green onions, thinly sliced
1 teaspoon finely grated fresh
  gingerroot
2 lemongrass stalks, thinly sliced

2 skinless chicken breast fillets, cut
  into ¾-inch cubes
¼ pound shiitake mushrooms, sliced
2 tablespoons soy sauce
1½ cups cooked basmati rice

1 Trim the banana leaves to 8-inch squares; set aside.
2 Heat the oil in a large skillet and sauté the green onions, gingerroot, and lemongrass for 2–3 minutes. Add the chicken and mushrooms, and stir-fry for 2 minutes. Add the soy sauce and cooked rice, and cook, stirring, for 1 minute.
3 Divide the mixture between the banana leaves, and fold over to enclose the filling; secure the parcels with bamboo skewers or twine. Place in a bamboo steamer over a wok, or in a metal steamer, and steam for 15 minutes.
4 Serve on warmed plates, allowing guests to open up their own parcels.

Note If banana leaves are unobtainable, lightly oiled baking parchment squares can be used instead, but the flavor won't be quite the same.

Banana leaves, lemongrass, green onions, gingerroot, and shiitake mushrooms give these aromatic parcels a distinctive character.

Chicken saltimbocca

4 slices prosciutto
12 large fresh sage leaves
4 skinless chicken breast fillets
salt and pepper
1 tablespoon olive oil

large knob of butter
1 red onion, sliced
dash of white wine
4 tablespoons crème fraîche

1 Lay the prosciutto slices on a worksurface, and place a sage leaf on each. Position the chicken breasts at an angle on top, and season with pepper. Top with another sage leaf, and wrap the chicken breasts in the prosciutto slices.
2 Heat the oil and butter in a heavy-based skillet, add the parcels, and fry for 2–3 minutes until lightly browned. Turn the parcels over and add the rest of the sage. Fry for 2 minutes until the sage leaves are frizzled; remove these with a slotted spoon and set aside.
3 Lower the heat, add the onion to the pan, and cook gently until softened. Turn the chicken parcels again. Add the wine, increasing the heat and stirring to deglaze the pan.
4 Lower the heat, stir in the crème fraîche and simmer gently for 2–3 minutes or until the chicken is cooked through. Serve garnished with the frizzled sage leaves.

These prosciutto and sage-flavored parcels are typically served with tagliatelle.

meat

Seared beef, physalis fruit, and onions

14 ounces small onions, peeled
3 tablespoons olive oil
2¼-pound piece beef fillet
salt and pepper
2 ounces physalis fruit
scant 1 cup Muscat de Beaume de
    Venise, or Sauternes

1 Preheat oven to 450°F. Put the onions in a roasting pan, add 1 tablespoon
of the oil, and toss to coat. Roast for 10 minutes.
2 Meanwhile, pat the beef fillet dry with paper towels, rub with 1 tablespoon
of oil, and season well.
3 Preheat a heavy-based skillet, add the beef, and brown on all sides
over a high heat for about 5 minutes. Transfer the beef to the roasting pan,
and roast with the onions for 15 minutes.
4 Toss the physalis fruit in the remaining 1 tablespoon oil. Add to the meat
and roast for another 7 minutes. Transfer the beef, onions, and physalis to a
warm serving dish, and leave to rest in a warm place for about 15 minutes.
5 Meanwhile, add the wine to the roasting pan, stirring to deglaze, and
bubble over a high heat for about 1 minute. Pour any meat juices that have
collected in the serving dish into the roasting pan, and heat through.
6 Carve the beef into medium-thick slices. Serve with physalis fruit and roast
onions on a bed of mashed potatoes and celeriac, drizzled with the meat juices.

Serve this tender beef, crowned with the
physalis fruit in their papery husks, on a
mound of mashed potatoes and celeriac, with
the sweet roast onions and rich meat juices.

Mustard steaks on mushrooms

Serves 2

2 fillet steaks, each 6 ounces
salt and pepper
2 teaspoons wholegrain mustard
2 teaspoons black olive paste
2 flat mushrooms, about 4 inches
  across

For the vegetable julienne

½ each red and yellow bell peppers,
  seeded and cut into fine strips
¼ small celeriac (approx. 2 ounces),
  cut into very fine strips

1 Preheat oven to 475°F. Using a sharp knife, score the steaks in a crisscross pattern at ½-inch intervals, cutting just less than halfway through depth.
2 Mix together the mustard and olive paste and spread over the meat and into the cuts. Place the steaks, mustard side down, on a foil-lined baking tray. Cook in a preheated high broiler for about 3 minutes.
3 Put the mushrooms, flat side up, on the baking tray. Turn the steaks over and carefully place on top of the mushrooms. Bake in the oven for 10 minutes, or until the mushrooms are cooked through; the steaks should still be pink in the middle. (For well done steaks cook for 2 to 3 minutes longer.)
4 Quickly toss together the vegetable julienne and pile on top of the steaks. Serve at once, with a salad.

A highly seasoned juicy steak cooked without extra fat and served with a crunchy julienne of vegetables.

Whiskey-braised beef with pecans

Illustrated on previous pages

4 lean, thick braising steaks, about
   1¾ pound in total
3–4 tablespoons seasoned flour
1 tablespoon olive oil
2 tablespoons butter
2 garlic cloves, thinly sliced
9 ounces shallots, peeled

2 fresh bay leaves, crushed
7 ounces lardoons, or bacon cut
   crosswise into thin strips
4 tablespoons whiskey
2 cups beef stock
⅛ cup pecans, halved
3 tablespoons chopped fresh parsley

1 Preheat oven to 180C/fan oven 160C/Gas 4. Coat the steaks with the seasoned flour.

2 Heat the oil and half the butter in a large skillet, and fry the steaks until sealed on both sides. Transfer to a shallow casserole.

3 Add the garlic, shallots, bay leaves, and half of the lardoons to the skillet; stir-fry until browned. Add the whiskey, bubble to reduce, then stir in the stock, scraping up any sediment from the base of the pan. Pour over the beef.

4 Cover and braise in the oven for two hours until tender. If preparing ahead, cool, then cover and chill for up to 3 days, or freeze.

5 To serve, defrost at cool room temperature overnight (if frozen). Reheat in a pan until piping hot. Fry the rest of the lardoons in the remaining butter until golden. Add the pecans and cook for a few minutes. Stir in the parsley.

6 Serve the beef casserole topped with the pecan mix. Accompany with creamy mashed potato and a green vegetable.

Braising steaks are cooked with a tot of whiskey, whole shallots, and smoky bacon, then served topped with a buttery mix of toasted pecans and crisp fried bacon.

Charred pepper and steak tacos

4 tablespoons olive oil

4 teaspoons Cajun spice seasoning

2 sirloin steaks, each 6 ounces, cut into strips

2 garlic cloves, crushed

4 yellow bell peppers, seeded and thinly sliced

3 red onions, sliced

12 small taco shells

two 8-ounce cans refried beans

4 tablespoons cilantro leaves, chopped

1¼ cups sour cream

1 Mix half the oil with the spice in a shallow dish. Add the steak and toss well; set aside.

2 Heat remaining oil in a wok, and stir-fry the garlic, peppers, and onions over a high heat for 8–10 minutes until lightly charred. Add the steak and stir-fry for 4–5 minutes.

3 Meanwhile warm the tacos and beans according to the packet instructions. Stir the chopped cilantro into the sour cream.

4 Spoon the beans into the taco shells. Top with the pepper mixture and some cream.

Taco shells are filled with steak strips, charred peppers, and refried beans, then topped with sour cream flavored with cilantro.

Fillet of beef teriyaki

1 pound piece beef fillet (from the tail end)

2 tablespoons sesame oil

4 tablespoons teriyaki marinade

olive oil, for brushing

vegetable oil, for frying

⅛ cup sliced pickled ginger, drained and dried

4 garlic cloves, peeled and thinly sliced

4–6 green onions, thinly sliced

1 Trim the beef of any fat or sinew, then place in a non-metallic dish. Spoon the sesame oil and teriyaki marinade over the meat, and turn to coat well. Cover and leave to marinate in the fridge for at least 4 hours, preferably overnight, turning the meat occasionally.

2 Bring to room temperature, lift the meat out of the marinade and pat dry.

3 Preheat broiler to high. Brush meat sparingly with olive oil and sear all over under the broiler for 2 minutes, turning as necessary. Turn down the heat to medium, and broil for another 20 minutes, turning 3 times.

4 Transfer the meat to a warm dish, cover with foil, and leave to rest in a warm place for 10 minutes.

5 Meanwhile, heat a ½-inch depth of oil in a skillet until a small piece of bread sizzles instantly as it touches the oil. Add the ginger, sliced garlic, and green onions, and fry until golden. Remove with a slotted spoon and drain on paper towels.

6 Serve the meat thinly sliced, drizzled with the meat juices and scattered with the ginger, garlic, and green onions.

This marinated, broiled fillet of beef is dark on the outside, but remains pink and moist inside. It is served with frizzled pickled ginger, green onions, and garlic.

Savoy cabbage and veal parcels

illustrated on previous pages

Serves 2

6 medium-size green Savoy cabbage
  leaves
2 teaspoons olive oil
2 shallots, finely chopped
1 garlic clove, crushed
10 ounces lean ground veal

1 teaspoon minced fresh rosemary
  leaves
4 juniper berries, crushed
⅝ cup well flavored chicken stock
1 cup fresh breadcrumbs
salt and pepper

1 Blanch the cabbage leaves in boiling water for 1–2 minutes. Drain and refresh in cold water, then drain and leave to dry on paper towels while preparing the filling.

2 Heat the oil in a pan, and fry the shallots and garlic for 5 minutes or until soft and translucent. Add the ground veal with the rosemary and crushed juniper berries; fry for 5–6 minutes until opaque. Add the stock, and continue cooking for 2–3 minutes.

3 Remove from the heat and add the breadcrumbs. Mix thoroughly, seasoning with pepper and a little salt if required.

4 Divide the veal mixture between the cabbage leaves. Fold in the sides of the leaves, then roll up loosely from the stem end. Secure each parcel with a wooden toothpick.

5 Put the cabbage parcels in a steamer, and steam for 8–10 minutes until the cabbage is tender and the filling is piping hot. Serve with a fresh tomato sauce.

Note Use pork instead of veal for the filling, but, to ensure a low-fat dish, make sure you buy lean pork tenderloin and grind it yourself.

Cabbage leaves envelop a tasty veal stuffing flavored with shallots, rosemary, and juniper—perfect with a fresh tomato sauce.

Mediterranean veal rolls

2 large veal scallops, each about
  6 ounces
For the stuffing
⅝ cup sun-dried eggplant slices
2 canned or bottled red bell peppers,
  drained

olive oil, for brushing
salt and pepper
1 buffalo mozzarella cheese, about
  5 ounces, sliced
handful of fresh basil leaves

1 For the stuffing, soak the eggplant slices in tepid water for 20 minutes.
Drain and pat dry with paper towels.
2 Put the veal scallops between sheets of waxed paper, and bat out thinly,
without tearing the meat.
3 Lay the peppers on top of each scallop, followed by the eggplant slices.
Brush with olive oil, season with salt and pepper, then cover with the sliced
mozzarella and basil leaves.
4 Preheat broiler to medium. Roll the veal scallops up from the longest side,
enclosing the filling. Secure with toothpicks and brush with olive oil. Broil
for 20 minutes, gradually turning the parcels to ensure even cooking.
5 Serve cut into slices, with a salad.

Note To barbecue, cook the veal rolls over medium coals for 15–20 minutes,
turning from time to time.

Flattened veal escalopes rolled around a tasty
stuffing of mozzarella, capsicums, sun-dried
eggplant, and basil.

Venison in coppa with chestnuts

Serves 4–6

1 teaspoon black mustard seeds
1 teaspoon juniper berries
1 teaspoon black peppercorns
1¼-pound piece venison fillet
salt
1¾ cup shelled fresh chestnuts
   (in skins)

1 tablespoon oil
¼ pound coppa (20 thin slices) or
   thinly sliced pancetta
scant ½ cup fruity red wine
knob of unsalted butter

1 Coarsely grind the mustard seeds, juniper, and peppercorns with a pestle and mortar. Rub the mixture all over the venison. Wrap tightly in plastic wrap; refrigerate 24 hours.

2 Bring meat to room temperature 1 hour before cooking, and season lightly with salt. Preheat oven to 425°F.

3 Pierce the skin of each chestnut, then put in a shallow roasting dish and toss with the oil. Season with salt, and roast for 5 minutes.

4 Lay the coppa or pancetta slices overlapping on waxed paper to form a rectangle, large enough to wrap around the venison. Lay the venison on the long edge, and, with the aid of the paper, roll the coppa around it to enclose. Wrap in oiled foil and roast with the chestnuts for 15 minutes.

5 Unwrap the venison, pour the juices into a small pan, then roast for another 5 minutes until the coppa is slightly crisp. Transfer to a serving dish, cover loosely, and rest in a warm place for 15 minutes; continue to roast the chestnuts during this time.

6 Add the wine to the meat juices and boil for 1 minute. Stir in the butter. Carve the meat, and serve with the chestnuts and glaze.

Venison is marinated overnight with juniper and mustard, then wrapped in coppa (Italian cured pork) and roasted with chestnuts.

Mahogany duck breasts with fruity salsa

4 duck breasts, each 6–7 ounces
salt and pepper
For the salsa
1 small eating apple

2 slices fresh pineapple
2 tablespoons dried cranberries
finely grated rind and juice of
  ½ lemon, or to taste

1 Pat the duck breasts dry with paper towels. Score the fat in a crisscross pattern, and rub with plenty of salt. Set aside.
2 Core and finely dice the apple. Finely dice the pineapple and mix with the cranberries and apple. Add lemon juice and rind to taste, and season with salt and pepper.
3 Preheat broiler to medium. Place the duck breasts, skin side down, on the broiler rack, and broil for 1 minute to sear the underside.
4 Turn the duck breasts over, and broil under the medium heat for 10 minutes. Reduce the heat to low, and continue to cook for another 10 minutes until the skin is dark brown; the flesh should be just rosy pink.
5 Slice the duck breasts, and serve accompanied by the fruity salsa.

Note To barbecue, cook the duck breasts flesh side down for 1 minute to seal. Turn over and cook for 10 minutes, dowsing any flames with water, as the fat can catch and ignite. Lift the barbecue rack away from the heat source a little, and continue to cook for another 10 minutes.

Duck breasts are broiled slowly until the skin is mahogany brown, then served with a zesty salsa of apple, pineapple, dried cranberries, and lemon.

Duck with caramelized orange and Campari

1 oven-ready duck, about 4 pounds
1 scant cup sugar
juice of 1 orange
3 tablespoons Campari
1 small onion, peeled
5 large fresh rosemary sprigs
salt
1 small orange, cut into slices
⅝ cup well flavored duck or chicken
  stock

1 Set the duck on a rack in the sink, and pour 2 saucepans of boiling water over it. Drain and let dry on paper towels in a cool place for 30 minutes, or hang the duck so air can circulate around it (to firm up the skin).
2 Preheat oven to 425°F. Put the sugar, orange juice, and 2 tablespoons Campari in a heavy-based pan on a low heat until the sugar is dissolved. Bring to the boil; simmer for 5 minutes or until syrupy.
3 Prick the duck skin all over. Put the onion and 1 rosemary sprig into the cavity. Set the duck on a rack in a roasting tin containing ¾ cup water. Roast for 20 minutes.
4 Brush the duck with some of the syrup and sprinkle with salt. Roast for another 30 minutes. Brush with more syrup and roast for another 30 minutes, lowering setting to 400°F if over-browning.
5 Dip orange slices in remaining syrup, and lay on the duck breast with the rosemary. Brush all over with syrup, and roast for a final 30 minutes or until the duck is cooked.
6 Transfer to a platter, cover loosely, and rest in a warm place for 15 minutes. Pour off fat from roasting pan, then place over a medium heat. Add stock and remaining Campari, stirring to deglaze. Add any remaining syrup and heat through. Serve with the duck.

Barbecued lamb with salmoriglio sauce

Serves 4–6

2 racks of lamb, each with 6–7
  cutlets
salt and pepper
olive oil, for brushing

For the salmoriglio sauce

¾ cup extra-virgin olive oil
juice of 1 large or 2 small lemons
2 teaspoons dried oregano
2 garlic cloves, finely chopped
2 tablespoons chopped fresh parsley

1 Trim the lamb of excess fat, but retain a thin covering to keep the meat moist during cooking. Rub all over with salt and pepper, and lightly brush with olive oil.

2 To make the sauce, whisk all of the ingredients together in a bowl until well combined and thick.

3 Preheat broiler to medium. Lay the racks of lamb down, fat side up, in the broiler pan, and broil for 15–20 minutes, checking frequently to make sure that the fat doesn't catch.

4 As soon as the meat is cooked, transfer to a warmed dish and pour the sauce over. Cover and leave to rest in a warm place for 10 minutes. Serve the lamb, cut into double cutlets, with the sauce spooned over.

Note Dried oregano is preferred to fresh here, for its intense, sweet flavor.

Racks of lamb are broiled to perfection, then drenched in a Sicilian sauce of lemon, garlic, oregano, and olive oil—to bring all the scents of southern Italy to your kitchen.

Loin of lamb with mushrooms and nuts

1½–2 pounds boned loin of lamb
salt and pepper
1 tablespoon olive oil
2 shallots, minced
1 garlic clove, crushed
6 ounces mushrooms, diced
1 small celery stalk, minced

½ cup cooked, peeled chestnuts (fresh or vacuum packed), roughly chopped
1 teaspoon paprika
¾ cup walnuts, finely chopped
½ cup fresh breadcrumbs
2 tablespoons vin de noix (walnut aperitif) or dry sherry

1 Cut away any skin and excess fat from the joint, leaving a thin coating. Score this in a crisscross pattern, and rub with seasoning.

2 For the stuffing, heat the oil in a pan, and fry the shallots and garlic until transparent. Add the mushrooms and cook gently until softened and all moisture is evaporated.

3 Add the celery, chestnuts, and paprika and cook for 2–3 minutes, then add the walnuts, breadcrumbs, aperitif, and 1 tablespoon water. Season to taste and let cool slightly. Preheat oven to 375°F.

4 Turn the meat flesh side up, and spread with the stuffing. Roll up and tie with string at 1-inch intervals. Place on a trivet in a roasting pan and roast for 1¼–1½ hours, or 2 hours for well done meat.

5 Leave the lamb to rest in a warm place for 10 minutes before carving.

A tasty chestnut and mushroom stuffing accentuates the sweet taste of the lamb.

Lamb with Chinese Spices

2 teaspoons sunflower oil

1 pound 2 ounces lean lamb fillet,
 cut into chunks

1 tablespoon fresh gingerroot
 julienne (fine sticks)

1 teaspoon Chinese five-spice powder

4 tablespoons Chinese rice wine or
 dry sherry

4 tablespoons dark soy sauce

3 tablespoons clear honey

8-ounce can water chestnuts,
 drained

2 leeks, sliced on the diagonal

1 large red bell pepper, cored, seeded
 and cut into diamonds

shredded green onion, to garnish
 (optional)

1 Heat the oil in a large heavy-based pan or flameproof casserole. Add the lamb and ginger and stir-fry until the meat is evenly colored. Sprinkle with the five-spice powder, then stir in the wine or sherry, soy sauce, honey, and water chestnuts. Bring to a simmer.

2 Cover the pan with a tight-fitting lid, and simmer over a gentle heat for 20 minutes.

3 Stir in the leeks and red pepper, then cover and cook for another 40 minutes, until the meat and vegetables are tender.

4 If preparing ahead, cool, cover and refrigerate for up to 2 days, or freeze.

5 To serve, defrost at cool room temperature overnight (if frozen). Reheat in a pan until piping hot.

6 Serve topped with shredded green onion, if wished. Accompany with rice or noodles, tossed with bean sprouts and steamed shredded sugar-snap peas.

Variation Replace the water chestnuts with an 8-ounce can sliced bamboo shoots. Serve sprinkled with toasted cashew nuts.

Rich soy sauce, honey, and the star anise in Chinese five-spice powder add intriguing flavors to this casserole.

Lamb stuffed with dates and spices

8 tablespoons olive oil

2 onions: 1 chopped, 1 finely sliced

2 plump garlic cloves: 1 crushed, 1 cut into slivers

large pinch of saffron strands

¼ teaspoon ground cinnamon

1 teaspoon ground cumin

salt and pepper

2 pieces preserved lemon, rinsed and finely chopped, or finely grated rind of 2 lemons

8 large dates, stoned and finely chopped

3–4 tablespoons chopped fresh cilantro leaves

3-pound leg of lamb, part boned (see note)

2 cinnamon sticks, broken

1 Heat 4 tablespoons oil in a heavy-based skillet and fry the chopped onion and crushed garlic until soft and golden. Add the saffron, cinnamon, cumin, and seasoning; stir well. Take off the heat, and add the lemon and dates. Stir to mix, and set aside until cold.

2 Mix the fresh cilantro into the stuffing, and use to stuff the lamb. Secure with skewers or sew up the stuffed pocket.

3 Preheat oven to 400°F. Make small incisions in the skin of the lamb, and insert the garlic slivers. Put in a roasting pan and brush with 2 tablespoons oil. Season well and surround with the cinnamon sticks.

4 Roast for 1 hour 20 minutes, basting from time to time. Transfer to a warm platter, cover loosely, and rest in a warm place for 15 minutes. Meanwhile, fry the sliced onion in the remaining oil until golden and crisp.

5 Serve the lamb topped with the fried onion and cinnamon sticks.

Note Part-boning leg of lamb to give a pocket for the stuffing is not difficult. Given notice, your butcher should to do it for you.

Thai-style lamb shanks

4 lamb shanks

1 tablespoons vegetable oil

2 large onions, minced

2 tablespoons Thai green curry paste

2 tablespoons lemongrass, finely
chopped

1 teaspoon ground cumin

1 teaspoon ground coriander

15-ounce can coconut milk

2¼ cups vegetable stock

3 tablespoons chopped cilantro leaves
salt and pepper

To garnish
cilantro leaves or finely sliced chile

1 Preheat oven to 425°F. Place the lamb shanks in a roasting pan, and roast for 40 minutes, turning them halfway through cooking.

2 Lift out the lamb shanks, drain off all of the fat, then transfer to a casserole in which they fit snugly. Lower the oven setting to 375°F.

3 Heat the oil in another pan, add the onions, and sauté until light golden. Add the curry paste, lemongrass, cumin, and coriander, and stir-fry for 1 minute. Add the coconut milk, stock, and chopped cilantro.

4 Pour this mixture over the lamb shanks, cover, and cook in the oven for 2½ hours until the meat is very tender. Check the seasoning of the sauce.

5 To serve, place each lamb shank in a warmed shallow serving bowl. Spoon some of the sauce over, and scatter with fresh cilantro or sliced chile. Serve with Thai jasmine rice and a steamed green vegetable, such as bok choi.

These succulent shanks of lamb are subtly flavored with coconut milk and Thai spices and baked until meltingly tender.

Baked eggplants with minted lamb

4 eggplants, each about ⅓ pound
10 ounces thin cut lean lamb fillet
salt and pepper
1 red onion, thinly sliced
2 tablespoons shredded fresh mint
  leaves

a little oil, for brushing (optional)
For the minted yogurt
scant 1 cup low-fat yogurt
1–2 tablespoons finely shredded
  fresh mint
1 garlic clove, crushed (optional)

1 Preheat a baking tray in the oven at 400°F. Cut each eggplant lengthwise into 5 slices, but not quite right through.

2 Season the lamb with salt and pepper and insert a slice into each eggplant slit, with some onion and shredded mint. Brush sparingly with oil and loosely wrap each eggplant in foil.

3 Place the parcels on the baking tray and bake for 45 minutes to 1 hour until the eggplant is tender through to the center.

4 Meanwhile, mix the yogurt with the mint, salt, and garlic if using. Chill until required.

5 Serve the baked eggplants hot, accompanied by the minted yogurt and basmati rice or steamed couscous.

Tasty eggplants are slit and filled with slices of lean lamb fillet and aromatic flavorings, then baked to create a delicious, healthful meal. Minted, garlicky yogurt is the perfect complement.

Rabbit in wine with olives and oregano

1¾ pounds boneless rabbit portions, cut into large chunks
4 tablespoons seasoned flour
2–3 tablespoons olive oil
9 ounces large shallots, peeled and quartered
2 large garlic cloves, crushed

9 ounces large button mushrooms, halved
1¼ cups dry white wine
⅝ cup chicken stock
¾ cup green olives
2 tablespoons chopped fresh oregano
salt and pepper

1 Coat the rabbit pieces in the seasoned flour. Heat the oil in a flameproof casserole, and fry the rabbit in batches until golden on all sides; remove with a slotted spoon. Add the shallots, garlic, and mushrooms to the pan; stir-fry for 3 minutes.

2 Pour in the wine and stock, return the rabbit pieces, and stir in the olives and oregano. Cover tightly and simmer for about 30 minutes until the rabbit is tender. Taste and adjust the seasoning.

3 If preparing ahead, cool, cover and refrigerate for up to 2 days, or freeze.

4 To serve, defrost at cool room temperature overnight (if frozen). Reheat in a flameproof casserole or heavy-based pan until piping hot. Serve with creamy mashed potatoes and a green vegetable.

Make this delicious wine-enriched casserole in advance to allow time for the flavors to fully develop.

Jamaican jerk pork chops

4 green onions, minced
2 red chiles, seeded and chopped
3 tablespoons vegetable oil
1 teaspoon allspice
2 tablespoons light muscovado sugar

2 tablespoons vinegar
2 teaspoons fresh thyme leaves
salt and pepper
4 pork loin chops, each about
   7 ounces

1 Put the green onions, chiles, oil, allspice, sugar, vinegar, and thyme leaves in a food processor. Season well and process until well blended.
2 Make 3–4 shallow slashes on both sides of each pork chop, and lay in a shallow, nonmetallic dish. Pour the jerk mixture over the chops and turn them to coat thoroughly. Cover and then leave to marinate in a cool place for 1 hour.
3 Preheat the broiler to medium high. Transfer the chops to the broiler rack and broil for 5–7 minutes on each side, or until the meat is tender, basting them occasionally.
4 Serve the broiled chops accompanied by baked sweet potatoes and an avocado, tomato, and red onion salad.

This traditional Jamaican recipe, usually made with chicken on the bone, works well with pork chops, too. It is also a great recipe for a barbecue.

Crisp roast stuffed shoulder of pork

Serves 4–6

3 pounds boneless shoulder of pork,
  with scored rind
⅝ cup pitted prunes, preferably Agen
4 tablespoons calvados or marsala
grated rind and juice of 1 orange
coarse salt and pepper
1 teaspoon clear honey

1 Soak the prunes in the calvados for 3–4 hours. Drain, reserving the liquor.
2 Preheat oven to 425°F. Open out the rolled joint of pork, and rub about
2 teaspoons salt into the slits of the scored rind.
3 Turn the joint over, spoon the prunes onto the flesh, and sprinkle with
the orange rind.
4 Roll up the meat and secure with string, tied at 1-inch intervals. Put the
meat in a roasting pan and add 4 tablespoons water to prevent the fat from
spluttering. Roast for about 20 minutes until the rind is crisp.
5 Reduce oven setting to 350°F. Roast for another 1½ hours, adding a little
more water as needed.
6 Lift the meat onto a warm serving dish and rest in a warm place for
10 minutes. Skim off the fat from the roasting juices, then add the reserved
calvados, orange juice, and honey. Stir to scrape up the sediment, and boil
to reduce slightly, to a glaze; season.
7 Carve the pork into thick slices; serve with the meat glaze.

Succulent roast pork flavored with juicy
prunes and a hint of calvados. For added
texture, ask the butcher to score the rind
and fat as shown.

Pork and rosemary skewers

1 pound pork tenderloin
4 fresh rosemary sprigs, leaves only
3 tablespoons balsamic vinegar
2 tablespoons sun-dried tomato paste

4 tablespoons olive oil
salt and pepper
lime wedges, to serve

1 Presoak 8 wooden kebab skewers in cold water for 20 minutes.
2 Trim the pork of any membrane, then cut lengthwise into 16 thin strips.
3 Pound the rosemary leaves with the balsamic vinegar, sun-dried tomato paste, olive oil, salt, and pepper, using a pestle and mortar. Transfer to a dish. Add the pork strips and turn to coat. Cover and leave to marinate in the fridge for at least 1 hour.
4 Preheat broiler to high. Thread 2 pork strips in a zigzag fashion onto each of the skewers. Lay on a foil-lined broiler pan, and broil for 2–3 minutes each side, or until browned on all sides and cooked through.
5 Serve with lime wedges and a salad.

Variation Use stripped rosemary branches for the kabob skewers. Strip the leaves from 8 woody stems, leaving about 1 inch intact at one end. Thread the pork onto the stems, and broil as above.

Note To barbecue, cook over hot coals for about 2 minutes per side.

Strips of pork fillet are marinated in crushed rosemary, balsamic vinegar, and sun-dried tomato paste, then threaded zigzag fashion onto skewers and broiled.

Crusted roast loin of pork

Illustrated on previous pages

Serves 6–8

3-pound loin of pork, with 6–8 bones

1 tablespoon balsamic vinegar

4 teaspoons caraway seeds, roughly crushed

2 teaspoons white peppercorns, roughly crushed

3 teaspoons Malden sea salt

9 sprigs of fresh bay leaves

2 tablespoons olive oil

1 Tie the meat with string to make sure the bones stand upright. Rub well with balsamic vinegar, and leave to stand for 20 minutes. Preheat oven to 400°F.

2 Mix caraway, white pepper and salt together, and press over the meat. Lay 1 bay sprig in a shallow roasting pan. Stand the pork loin on top and drizzle with the oil. Roast for 15 minutes, basting with the pan juices occasionally.

3 Push the rest of the bay leaf sprigs under the string, and roast for another 20 minutes.

4 Lower oven setting to 350°F. Cover the meat loosely with foil, and roast for another 30 minutes or until cooked through. To test, insert a skewer into the middle; the juices should run clear.

5 Lift meat onto a dish, cover loosely, and allow to rest in a warm place for 15 minutes. Meanwhile, pour off the fat from the pan, then add 3 tablespoons water, stirring to deglaze.

6 Scatter the loin with the remaining salt, and serve cut into thick slices with the bone attached and the pan juices spooned over. Serve with baked baby beets and potatoes.

Note Buy a whole pork loin with 6–8 chops and ask your butcher to remove all skin, fat, and connecting bone, leaving the thin individual bone attached to each chop.

Pork steaks with sloe gin

4 pork leg steaks, trimmed of fat
2 tablespoons well seasoned flour
2 tablespoons butter
4 juniper berries, finely chopped
scant ½ cup sloe gin

⅝ cup heavy cream
1 tablespoon finely chopped fresh
  flat leaf parsley
salt and pepper

1 Toss the pork steaks in the seasoned flour to coat lightly on both sides, shaking off excess.
2 Melt the butter in a large skillet, and scatter in the juniper berries. Add the pork steaks; fry for about 3 minutes each side until just cooked and turning golden.
3 Pour in the sloe gin, and allow to bubble until reduced by half.
4 Lift out the pork steaks and transfer to hot serving plates; keep warm. Add the cream to the pan juices with the chopped parsley, and stir to make a sauce, scraping up any sediment from the base of the pan. Season with salt and pepper to taste. Bring to a simmer, stirring.
5 Pour this sauce over the pork steaks, and serve at once with new potatoes, broccoli and sugar-snap peas.

Note Sloe gin is available from some liquor stores. Alternatively, you can make your own in the fall by macerating sloes, picked in the countryside, with gin and sugar.

Pork steaks are cooked with a hint of juniper, then served in a rich creamy, sloe gin sauce for a special supper.

Chile pork and cheese burgers

1 pound 10 ounces ground pork
2 garlic cloves, crushed
2 tablespoons sweet chile sauce
3 green onions, finely chopped
3 tablespoons chopped fresh
  cilantro leaves

salt and pepper
2 ounces Gorgonzola cheese
oil, for brushing
To serve
4 English muffins or burger buns,
  split and toasted

1 Put the ground pork, garlic, chile sauce, green onions, and chopped cilantro in a bowl. Season with salt and pepper, and mix thoroughly until the mixture holds together, Divide into 4 equal portions, and then shape into patties.

2 Cut the blue cheese into 4 cubes, and mold each portion of pork mixture around a cheese cube to enclose. Flatten to form fat burgers.

3 Preheat broiler to medium. Brush the pork burgers with a little oil. Place on the broiler rack, and cook under the medium heat for about 7 minutes each side until cooked through. (Alternatively, you can barbecue the burgers over medium-hot coals allowing about 6 minutes per side.)

4 Serve at once, on toasted English muffins or burger buns, with French fries, ketchup, and mustard, if you like.

Note Bring meat to room temperature before broiling, and preheat the broiler for at least 10 minutes. Temperature settings of broilers vary considerably, so treat suggested cooking times as guidelines only. if you are barbecuing rather than broiling, remember to light the coals well ahead, and wait until they are "white hot" before starting to cook. Always test meat to make sure it is properly cooked to your liking.

These spicy burgers reveal a hidden pocket of melted blue cheese when cut open.

Sausage and apple pie with potato crust

For the pastry

1⅝ cup self-rising flour

¼ teaspoon salt

¼ teaspoon pepper

1½ sticks (12 tablespoons) butter, diced

1 cup cold mashed potato

For the filling

1 tbsp olive oil

2 onions, chopped

2 cooking apples, about ¾ pound, peeled, cored, and chopped

2 pounds low-fat pork sausages, skinned

1½ cups canned corn, drained

¼ teaspoon grated fresh nutmeg

½ teaspoon ground black pepper

½ teaspoon salt

1 large egg, beaten

1 For the pastry, sift the flour and seasoning into a bowl, then rub in the butter until the mixture resembles breadcrumbs. Add the potato and work to a soft dough. Wrap in plastic wrap and chill while making the filling.

2 Heat the oil in a pan, and fry onions until beginning to soften. Add apples and cook for 2–3 minutes until starting to soften, then turn into a bowl.

3 Add the sausage meat, corn, nutmeg, seasoning, and beaten egg. Mix thoroughly with clean hands and then transfer to a shallow 10-inch pie dish.

4 Lightly press out the pastry with your hands on a lightly floured surface until large enough to cover the pie. Carefully lift the filling over, trim the edges, and make a slit in the top of the pie. Chill for up to 24 hours until ready to bake.

5 Preheat a baking tray in the oven at 375°F. Place the pie on the baking tray and bake for 1–1¼ hours, covering lightly with foil if the pastry appears to be over-browning. Serve hot, with seasonal vegetables.

This potato pastry has a lovely light, buttery texture. For best results, use low-fat rather than traditional sausages for the filling.

Maple and mustard glazed ham

Serves 6–8

1 bone-in ham, about 6½ pounds

⅝ cup maple syrup

⅛ cup superfine sugar

2 teaspoons Dijon or honey mustard

15 cloves

1 Preheat oven to 350°F. Line a large roasting pan with a sheet of extra-wide foil, allowing plenty of overhang at each end. Lay another sheet of foil crosswise on top, to overhang the sides of the pan generously. Put the ham in the center and bring the ends of the foil up over the top. Fold together to seal well and make a roomy tent over the ham. Bake in the oven, allowing 30 minutes per pound.

2 Put the maple syrup and sugar in a small heavy-based pan, and heat gently until the sugar is dissolved. Add the mustard and simmer until syrupy.

3 Drain off the juices from the ham. Increase oven setting to 425°F. Cut a zigzag pattern in the skin at the narrow end of the joint, to about 3 inches from the end. Remove the skin from the rest of the ham, leaving a layer of fat. Score the fat in a lattice pattern, at 1-inch intervals.

4 Brush the whole joint with half of the syrup. Roast, uncovered, for 5 minutes per pound, until glazed and golden, brushing with the remaining syrup and studding each lattice with a clove halfway through this time.

5 If serving hot, allow to rest in a warm place for 20 minutes; if serving cold, leave to cool completely.

Note Ask your butcher for the knuckle end to get a traditional ham shape. Unless it is mild cure or presoaked, you will need to soak it for 24 hours before cooking, otherwise the meat will be too salty.

This traditional whole baked ham is equally good served hot with creamy mash and peas, or cold with salads.

vegetables and salads

Caramelized leeks on sweet potato rösti

2¼ pounds sweet potatoes
1 egg, beaten
4 tablespoons olive oil
2 tablespoons butter
10 ounces shallots, peeled and split
9 ounces baby leeks, halved

1 teaspoon minced fresh sage leaves
1½ teaspoons sugar
salt and pepper
1 tablespoon marsala (optional)
sage leaves, to garnish

1 Preheat oven to 375°F. Coarsely grate the sweet potatoes, mix with the beaten egg, and season well. Shape the grated potato into 12 heaped spoonfuls on 2 oiled baking sheets, spacing apart. Flatten slightly, and bake for 5–8 minutes until golden. Turn over and bake for another 5 minutes.
2 Heat 2 tablespoons oil and half of the butter in a heavy based pan over a high heat until sizzling. Add the shallots, lower the heat, cover, and cook for about 8 minutes, until soft and evenly browned. Remove with a slotted spoon and place in a warm dish.
3 Heat the remaining oil and butter in the pan over a high heat until sizzling. Add the leeks with the chopped sage, and cook in the same way, for about 5 minutes.
4 Increase heat and return shallots to the pan. Add the sugar, seasoning, and marsala if using, and cook, stirring, until caramelized. Arrange the röstis and vegetables on warmed plates, allowing 3 röstis per person. Serve at once, garnished with sage.

Note For convenience, you can prepare the röstis in advance. Reheat in oven at 400°F for 10 minutes to serve.

These tasty rosti are an ideal light main course for vegetarian entertaining.

Thai mushroom and snow pea salad

Illustrated on previous pages

10 ounces snow peas, halved
3 tablespoons vegetable oil
2 garlic cloves, minced
4 shallots, minced
1 pound 2 ounces portobello
    mushrooms, stalks removed,
    thickly sliced
2 teaspoons clear honey

juice of 2 limes
2 teaspoons lemongrass, minced
2 teaspoons Thai fish sauce
1 hot red chile, finely sliced
3 tablespoons fresh torn basil leaves
3 tablespoons fresh torn cilantro
    leaves
salt and pepper

1 Cook the snow peas in boiling water for 2 minutes until just tender. Drain and set aside.

2 Heat oil in a wok, and stir-fry the garlic and shallots for 2 minutes. Add the mushrooms and stir-fry for 5 minutes. Add the snow peas, and stir-fry for 1 minute. Turn into a bowl.

3 Mix the honey, lime juice, lemongrass, and fish sauce together, then add to the salad with the chile and herbs. Toss well and check the seasoning. Serve the salad at room temperature.

A delicious salad, fragrantly flavored with lemongrass, chile, and lime juice.

Pan-fried feta cheese salad

6 tablespoons instant polenta
1 teaspoon ground cumin
1 pound feta cheese, cut into
   12 slices
2 eggs, beaten
8 tablespoons olive oil
1 head Boston lettuce, separated
   into leaves
1 large avocado, peeled, stoned,
   and sliced

4 vine-ripened tomatoes, sliced
2 shallots, thinly sliced
For the dressing
1 large garlic clove, minced
juice of 2 limes
4 tablespoons clear honey
   (preferably acacia)
2 tablespoons chopped fresh mint

1 Mix polenta with cumin. Dip the feta slices in the egg, then coat in the spiced polenta.

2 Heat half the oil in a large skillet and fry the feta in batches on both sides until crisp.

3 Mix the dressing ingredients with the remaining oil and 2 tablespoons water.

4 Pile the lettuce, avocado, tomatoes, and shallots into bowls, and top with the fried feta.

5 Wipe any polenta from the pan, then pour in the dressing and heat until bubbling. Pour over the salad and serve, with warm pitas.

Hot slices of feta with a crisp spicy coating, served on a tomato and avocado salad.

Sri Lankan vegetable curry

large wedge pumpkin (approx.
　1¼ pounds), peeled and seeded
½-pound potato, peeled
2 tablespoons vegetable oil
1 onion, minced
1–2 cinnamon sticks
2 garlic cloves, minced
2 green chiles, seeded and finely
　sliced
¼ teaspoon turmeric
1 teaspoon fenugreek seeds
¼ pound green beans, trimmed
　and halved
8–10 fresh curry leaves
15-ounce can coconut milk
salt and pepper

1 Cut pumpkin and potato into 1-inch cubes. Heat the oil in a large pan, and gently fry the onion with the cinnamon until soft.
2 Add the garlic, chiles, turmeric, and fenugreek seeds. Cook, stirring, for 1 minute.
3 Add the pumpkin, potato, and green beans and fry, stirring, for 1–2 minutes. Add curry leaves, coconut milk, and ⅝ cup water.
4 Bring to the boil, then lower the heat, and simmer, covered, for about 15 minutes. Season to taste, and serve with rice.

A coconut based curry with pumpkin, potatoes, and green beans, flavored with fenugreek seeds and curry leaves.

Broiled eggplant terrine

Illustrated on previous pages

2 large eggplants, about 1½ pounds
  in total
6–8 tablespoons extra-virgin olive oil
salt and pepper
4 plum tomatoes, cored and cut into
  ⅛-inch slices
⅝ cup black olive tapenade

18 fresh large basil leaves,
  stalks removed
For the vinaigrette dressing
2 teaspoons cider vinegar
2 tablespoons olive oil
½ teaspoon Dijon mustard

1 Cut the eggplants into ⅛-inch slices. Preheat the broiler to high. Brush the
eggplant slices with oil, and season with salt and pepper. Broil in batches for
3–4 minutes each side or until golden, turning once. Drain on paper towels.
2 Line the base and sides of a 6½ x 4½ x 3-inch nonstick bread pan with
overlapping slices of eggplant. (Alternatively, use an ordinary bread pan
lined with plastic wrap.)
3 Arrange a layer of tomato slices in the tin. Spread a third of the tapenade
over the tomato, then scatter a third of the basil leaves over. Cover with a
layer of eggplant slices. Repeat these layers twice more, finally finishing
with a layer of eggplant. Cover the terrine with plastic wrap and chill in the
refrigerator for 2–4 hours.
4 For the dressing, put the ingredients in a screwtop jar, season with salt
and pepper, and shake well to emulsify.
5 To serve, unmold the terrine onto a board or plate, and cut into thick
slices. Serve drizzled with the dressing.

Serve this elegant terrine as a stylish
vegetarian lunch with toasted olive ciabatta.

Spinach, ricotta, and pistachio filo pie

Serves 6

8 large sheets filo pastry

For the filling

1 pound small, young spinach leaves

9 ounces ricotta cheese, drained

1 cup shelled pistachio nuts, finely chopped

⅝ cup sun-dried tomatoes, minced

2 tablespoons finely chopped fresh marjoram (optional)

salt and pepper

1 egg yolk, beaten

To assemble

1 egg white, beaten

6 tablespoons butter, melted

1 Grease a 10-inch springform cake pan or pizza pan.

2 For the filling, blanch the spinach in boiling water for 30 seconds. Drain, refresh in cold water, and drain well, squeezing out as much moisture as possible. Chop the spinach finely and place in a bowl.

3 Add the ricotta, pistachio nuts, sun-dried tomatoes, and marjoram, if using. Mix well and season, then stir in the egg yolk to bind the mixture.

4 Preheat oven to 425°F. Lay one sheet of filo on a clean surface; keep the rest wrapped to prevent it from drying. Take one-eighth of the filling and lay it along one long edge of the filo. Roll up to within ½ inch from the edge, to form a lip (for the next roll to sit on).

5 Curl the roll into a coil and place in the center of the pan. Brush the lip with egg white, then brush the top of the filo roll with melted butter.

6 Repeat with the rest of the filo and filling, positioning the rolls in the pan as you make them to form a continuous spiral. (The final roll will not need a lip.)

7 Brush the top of the filo pie with the remaining butter, and bake for 20–30 minutes until golden and crisp. Carefully unmould the pie onto a flat plate, and serve hot or cold, with a salad.

Serve this unusual coiled filo pie hot or cold, with a leafy salad.

Goat cheese and bacon gougère

4 slices rindless smoked bacon
1 stick (8 tablespoons) butter
⅝ cup water
generous ¾ cup bread flour
1 teaspoon mustard
4 large eggs, beaten
salt and pepper
¼ pound soft goat cheese, in pieces

For the filling
3 tablespoons olive oil
3 garlic cloves, crushed
1 pound zucchini, thickly sliced
1 large eggplant, cubed
15-ounce can chopped tomatoes
1 tablespoon chopped fresh oregano
1 teaspoon sugar
scant ½ cup pitted green olives

1 Preheat oven to 425°F. Grease 4 individual 1¼ cup soufflé dishes. Dry-fry the bacon in a pan until crisp, then cut into small pieces.

2 To make the choux pastry, put the butter and water in a heavy-based pan, and heat until the butter is melted and the mixture boils. Add the flour all at once, and beat vigorously over the heat for about 1 minute until the mixture leaves the side of the pan. Take off the heat and stir until lukewarm.

3 Add the mustard, then gradually beat in the eggs, until smooth. Stir in the bacon and season. Carefully fold in the cheese, so that it forms pockets through the mixture.

4 Divide the mixture between the soufflé dishes, and bake for 25 minutes until well risen and golden.

5 Meanwhile, prepare the filling. Heat the oil in a pan and fry the garlic, zucchini and eggplant until beginning to soften. Stir in tomatoes, oregano, sugar, and seasoning, Cover and simmer for 15 minutes.

6 Add the olives to the vegetables. Spoon some on top of the gougère; serve the remainder separately.

Goat cheese and crisp fried smoked bacon add a savory tang to choux pastry. For a vegetarian dish, omit the bacon.

Roasted eggplant and red rice salad

Illustrated on previous pages

2 medium eggplants, generous
  1 pound in total
2 tablespoons tahini paste
salt and pepper
1 tablespoon sesame seeds
2 red onions, cut into wedges

1 tablespoon olive oil
1 cup red Camargue rice
7 ounces radicchio, torn
handful of arugula leaves
a little walnut oil and lemon juice
  (optional)

1 Preheat oven to 425°F. Cut eggplants into 1½-inch cubes, brush with tahini, and place in a nonstick roasting pan. Season and sprinkle with sesame seeds.
2 Put the onion wedges in another roasting pan and sprinkle with olive oil.
3 Put both pans in the oven, and roast for about 40 minutes or until tender, swapping shelves halfway through cooking.
4 Meanwhile, put the rice in a pan with 2½ cups cold water. Bring to the boil, reduce heat, cover, and simmer for about 40 minutes until tender. Drain if necessary.
5 Allow the vegetables and rice to cool slightly, then gently toss together while still warm. Set aside to cool further.
6 Serve warm or cold on the radicchio and arugula, dressed with a little walnut oil and lemon juice, if liked.

A rustic dish of intriguing flavors and muted colors – delicious warm or cold—as a vegetarian main course.

Gado gado

9 ounces potatoes, halved if large

3 carrots, cut into ¼-inch slices

½ pound green beans, halved

¼ white or Savoy cabbage (approx. 9 ounces), cored and thinly shredded

1 small cucumber, thickly sliced

7 ounces bean sprouts

4 hard-boiled eggs, quartered

½ cup roasted peanuts, roughly chopped

For the dressing

1 tablespoon vegetable oil

1 small onion, minced

2 garlic cloves, minced

1 red chile, minced

generous ¾ cup crunchy peanut butter

⅞ cup coconut milk

⅝ cup water

1 tablespoon soy sauce

1 tablespoon tomato ketchup

1 Cook the potatoes in lightly salted water until just tender. Drain and leave until cool enough to handle, then peel and cut into ¼-inch slices.

2 Add the carrots to a pan of boiling salted water and blanch for 5 minutes; drain and refresh in cold water; drain thoroughly. Repeat with the green beans and cabbage, allowing 3–5 minutes blanching time for the beans, 3 minutes for the cabbage.

3 To make the dressing, heat the oil in a heavy-based pan. Add the onion, garlic, and chile and cook gently for 5 minutes. Add the peanut butter, coconut milk, and water. Bring to the boil, stirring constantly. Lower the heat, then add the soy sauce and tomato ketchup. Remove from the heat, stir well, and leave to cool.

4 Arrange all of the vegetables and the hard-boiled eggs on a large serving platter in separate piles. Scatter the roasted peanuts over.

5 To serve, spoon some of the dressing over the eggs and vegetables. Serve the remainder separately.

This classic Indonesian salad is served with a creamy coconut and peanut dressing, spiked with garlic and chile.

Vegetable and goat cheese salad

7 ounces small, young leeks
5 ounces sugar-snap peas
10 ounces asparagus
⅛ cup pumpkin seeds
5 ounces firm goat cheese, cubed
pepper
a little walnut or olive oil (optional)

1 Cut the leeks into 1-inch lengths, put into a steamer, and steam for
2 minutes. Add the sugar-snaps, and cook for another 5 minutes. Transfer
both vegetables to a warm bowl; set aside.
2 Cut the asparagus into 2-inch pieces, and steam for 5 minutes or until just
tender. Add to the other vegetables.
3 Preheat a heavy-based skillet and dry-fry the pumpkin seeds for 2 minutes
until they begin to pop and brown slightly.
4 Arrange the vegetables in a serving dish. Top with the goat cheese,
pumpkin seeds and pepper. Drizzle with a little walnut or olive oil to serve,
if wished.

A delicious warm salad of asparagus, leeks,
and sugar-snap peas, topped with goat cheese
and toasted pumpkin seeds.

Butternut risotto with arugula

4 tablespoons pumpkin seeds
4 tablespoons butter
2 onions, minced
3 garlic cloves, thinly sliced
1¾ cups arborio or other risotto rice
5 cups chicken or vegetable stock
1 butternut squash, about 1¼ pounds, peeled, seeded, and cubed

⅝ cup extra-dry vermouth
4 ounces pecorino or Parmesan shavings
1 ounce arugula leaves
salt and pepper

1 Dry-fry the pumpkin seeds in a large skillet for 1 minute until they start to pop. Remove and set aside.
2 Melt the butter in the pan, and fry the onions and garlic for 5 minutes to soften. Add the rice, and stir to coat in the butter.
3 Pour in the boiling stock and boil for 5 minutes, stirring frequently.
4 Add the squash, vermouth, and 1¼ cups boiling water. Return to the boil, lower heat, and cook, stirring often, for 10 minutes until the rice and squash are just tender.
5 Add two-thirds of the cheese, half the arugula, and the pumpkin seeds. Season. Serve topped with the remaining arugula and cheese shavings.

Note For an authentic creamy texture, it is essential to use a risotto rice, such as arborio or carnaroli, rather than a long grain variety.

Butternut squash, toasted pumpkin seeds, peppery arugula leaves, and pecorino cheese make this a satisfying vegetarian meal.

Red pepper tagine with harissa

4 tablespoons olive oil

4 red bell peppers, cored, seeded, and roughly chopped

3 red onions, chopped

4 garlic cloves, crushed

½ teaspoon ground cumin

½ teaspoon ground coriander

½ teaspoon paprika

two 15-ounce cans chopped tomatoes

two 15-ounce cans red kidney beans

4 celery sticks, sliced

1 tablespoon harissa (see note)

1 teaspoon salt

3–4 tablespoons chopped fresh cilantro

3–4 tablespoons chopped fresh mint

mint or cilantro sprigs, to garnish

1 Heat the oil in a large pan. Add the red peppers, onions, and garlic, and fry, stirring, over a high heat until softened. Stir in the spices, and cook, stirring, for about 30 seconds to release their flavor.

2 Pour in the tomatoes. Drain the liquid from the kidney beans into the pan, then stir in the celery, harissa, and salt. Cover and simmer for 15 minutes or until the celery is just tender.

3 Stir in the kidney beans and heat through until simmering. If preparing ahead, allow to cool, then cover and chill for up to 2 days, or freeze.

4 To serve, defrost at cool room temperature overnight (if frozen). Reheat the tagine in a large pan until bubbling, and stir in the chopped cilantro and mint. Serve on a bed of steamed couscous, garnished with mint or cilantro.

Note Harissa is a fiery hot North African spice paste made from ground red bell peppers, chiles, onions, and spices. It is available in jars from some supermarkets and delicatessens.

Serve on a mound of fluffy couscous as a sustaining meal, with extra harissa for added spice, if you like.

Beet soufflés with chives

1 stick plus 1 tablespoon butter
1 ounce pecorino cheese, finely grated
½ cup all-purpose flour
2 cups milk
salt and white pepper
9 ounces beets, cooked and drained (see note)

½ pound soft goat cheese, finely crumbled
4 medium egg yolks
3 tablespoons finely snipped fresh chives
6 medium egg whites

1 Preheat oven to 375°F. Melt 4 tablespoons butter; dice the rest and set aside. Brush 4 individual 1¼-cup capacity soufflé dishes with melted butter and chill for 10 minutes. Brush with butter again and dust with the grated cheese.

2 Put the diced butter, flour, and milk in a pan, and whisk on a medium heat until smooth, thickened, and bubbling; season very generously (the whisked egg whites will dilute the flavor). Remove from the heat.

3 Dice 1 small beet and divide between the soufflé dishes, scattering a quarter of the crumbled goat cheese over.

4 Put the remaining beet in a blender or food processor with the sauce, and mix to a purée. Add egg yolks with the remaining goat cheese and process briefly until incorporated. Transfer to a bowl, and fold in the chives.

5 Whisk the egg whites in a clean bowl until they form peaks. Fold into the beet mixture, a little at a time.

6 Spoon the mix into the soufflé dishes to within ½ inch of the rim. Stand on a baking sheet and cook for 20–30 minutes until risen. Serve immediately.

Note Cook the beets, unpeeled, in simmering salted water for about 45 minutes, until tender. Drain and cool, then rub off the skin and dice the beets.

Serve as a sophisticated light lunch, with melba toast and a side salad.

Baked root layer cake

Illustrated on previous pages

¾ pound carrots
1 large (approx. ¾ pound) parsnip
1 large (approx. ¾ pound) celeriac
2 tablespoons clear honey

2 tablespoons lemon juice
6 tablespoons butter
salt and pepper
thyme sprigs, to garnish

1 Preheat oven to 400°F. Peel and coarsely grate the carrots, parsnip, and celeriac, using a hand grater or food processor fitted with a coarse grating disk, keeping each vegetable separate. Place in individual bowls.
2 Warm the honey, lemon juice, and butter in a small pan over a low heat until melted. Season with salt and pepper. Pour a third of this mixture over each vegetable, and mix well to coat.
3 Line a shallow 8-inch springform cake pan with non-stick baking parchment. Spoon the carrot into the tin, spread evenly, and press down gently. Repeat with the parsnip. Finish with the celeriac, pressing down gently as before.
4 Cover with buttered foil, and bake for 35 minutes, removing the foil for the final 10 minutes to brown the top.
5 Leave to stand for 10 minutes, then turn out and remove lining paper. Garnish with thyme, and serve cut into wedges.

This layered "cake" of carrot, parsnip, and celeriac is perfect with roast meat or game.

Roasted vegetables with thyme and lemon

¾ pound sweet potato, peeled
1 eggplant, trimmed
2 zucchini, cut into chunks
1 red bell pepper, halved, cored, and deseeded
1 small fennel bulb, halved and cored
1 small red onion, cut into wedges
1 tablespoon chopped fresh thyme, plus 3–4 sprigs

4 tablespoons olive oil
coarse sea salt and pepper
2 rosemary sprigs
To finish
finely grated zest of ½ lemon
2 tablespoons chopped fresh flat leaf parsley
¼ cup pine nuts, toasted
juice of ½ lemon, or to taste

1 Preheat the oven to 425°F. Cut the sweet potato into 1½-inch chunks; thickly slice the eggplant; cut the zucchini into chunks on the diagonal; cut the bell pepper into 1½-inch squares; cut the fennel into thin wedges. Put these vegetables into a large bowl with the onion wedges. Add the olive oil and chopped thyme, and toss well.

2 Transfer the vegetables to a large roasting pan, placing them in a single layer. Sprinkle with sea salt and pepper, then scatter the thyme and rosemary sprigs on top.

3 Roast for about 45 minutes until the vegetables are tender, stirring from time to time to ensure even browning. Meanwhile, mix together the lemon zest, parsley, and pine nuts,

4 Transfer the roasted vegetables to a warm serving dish, and scatter the parsley mixture over. Finish with a generous squeeze of lemon juice.

Serve as a light vegetarian main dish, or as an accompaniment to chargrilled meat, such as lamb chops and steaks.

Polenta with thyme-scented vegetables

5½ cups water

salt and pepper

1 stick plus 1 tablespoon butter, cut
   into cubes

2¾ cups quick-cook polenta

2 egg yolks, beaten

¼ pound pecorino or Parmesan
   cheese

8 tablespoons extra-virgin olive oil

1 onion, minced

4 garlic cloves, crushed

1 red pepper, cored, seeded, and
   chopped

4 fresh thyme sprigs

6 ounces small okra, tips trimmed

9 ounces patty pan, squash or
   zucchini, halved

2 large tomatoes, skinned and
   chopped

thyme sprigs, to garnish

1 To make the polenta, bring the water to the boil in a pan. Add salt and half of the butter. Take off the heat and pour in the polenta, whisking constantly. Continue to whisk over a low heat until thick. Off the heat, whisk in the egg yolks and two-thirds of the cheese. Tip onto a dampened baking tray, and spread to an even thickness, about ⅝ inch. Leave to cool. Melt remaining butter.

2 Heat 4 tablespoons oil in a large pan, and fry the onion and garlic until softened. Add the red pepper and thyme sprigs; cook for 5 minutes. Lift out vegetables with a slotted spoon.

3 Heat remaining oil in the pan, and stir-fry the okra over a high heat for 2 minutes. Add patty pans and cook, stirring, for 2 minutes. Add the onion mixture, tomatoes, and seasoning. Lower heat, and cook for about 4 minutes; the vegetables should retain a bite.

4 Preheat oven to 400°F. Cut polenta into triangles; arrange over-lapping on baking sheets. Brush with melted butter, scatter with remaining cheese, and bake for 10–20 minutes until golden. Serve topped with the vegetables and fresh thyme.

Serve as an accompaniment to broiled meats, or as a vegetarian main course.

Caramelized new potatoes with orange

Illustrated on previous pages

2 pounds new potatoes, scrubbed
salt and pepper
2 fresh mint sprigs
4 tablespoons butter
2 tablespoons fine-cut Seville orange
   marmalade
1 tablespoon finely chopped fresh
   mint

1 Add the potatoes to a large pan of boiling salted water with the mint
sprigs, and cook for 7–10 minutes, depending on size, until almost tender.
Drain well; discard the mint.
2 Melt the butter in a wide-based pan, add the potatoes, and shake the pan
to coat the potatoes in the butter.
3 Add the marmalade and heat gently to melt it, turning the potatoes to coat
well. Cook for about 15 minutes, stirring, until golden brown and caramelized.
4 Toss in the chopped mint and serve.

New potatoes with a sweet hint of marmalade
to partner duck, chicken, or pork.

Indian potato and corn salad

1½ pounds boiling potatoes, peeled
   and cut into 1-inch cubes
2 tablespoons vegetable oil
6 green onions, finely sliced
2 teaspoons cumin seeds
1 teaspoon hot paprika

2½ cups corn niblets, drained
juice of 1 lemon
½ teaspoon garam masala
3 tablespoons chopped fresh
   cilantro leaves
salt

1 Cook the potatoes in lightly salted water until tender. Drain and set aside.
2 Heat the oil in a large skillet, and stir-fry the onions for 1–2 minutes. Add
the cumin seeds; fry, stirring, for 30 seconds.
3 Add the paprika, potatoes, and corn. Heat through, then stir in the lemon
juice and garam masala. Take off the heat, and gently stir in the cilantro.
Season with salt and serve warm, or at room temperature.

Paprika, cumin, and lemon juice give this
unusual salad a piquant flavor.

Fennel, endive, and lime salad

Illustrated on previous pages

2 Florence fennel bulbs (with fronds)
¼ pound curly endive
For the dressing
finely grated rind and juice of
    2 limes
6 tablespoons extra-virgin olive oil
2 tablespoons finely shredded fresh
    basil

2 tablespoons finely diced pitted
    Greek black olives
2 sun-dried tomatoes in oil, drained
    and finely chopped
salt and pepper

1 Mix the dressing ingredients together in a large bowl and set aside.
2 Trim the fennel, discarding the stalks but reserving the feathery fronds.
Halve and core the bulbs, then finely slice, using a mandolin or very sharp
knife. Immediately toss the fennel slices in the dressing; leave to marinate
for 15 minutes.
3 Add the curly endive and reserved fennel fronds to the marinated fennel,
toss gently to mix, then transfer to a clean salad bowl. Serve immediately.

Note To prevent discoloration, toss the fennel in the dressing as soon as
it is sliced, and don't marinate the salad for longer than stated in the recipe.

Wafer-thin slices of fennel are marinated in a
tangy citrus dressing to soften, then combined
with crisp curly endive to make a refreshing
side salad.

Avocado and red chile salad

Serves 3–4
2 large or 3 small ripe avocados
2 bananas
2 tablespoons lemon juice
1 teaspoon finely minced red chile

½ cup walnuts, roughly chopped
salt and pepper
1 tablespoon finely shredded
  cilantro leaves

1 Peel the avocados and bananas, then cut into bite-size pieces, discarding the avocado stone. Place in a bowl.
2 Immediately toss with the lemon juice, chile, walnuts, seasoning, and cilantro. Serve at once, with wholewheat bread.

An unusual medley of flavors makes this a lively, nutritious salad.

desserts

Pecan and maple syrup baklava

Makes 12–20 squares
2 cups shelled pecans
generous ¼ cup light muscovado
  sugar

½ teaspoon ground mixed spice
14 ounces large filo pastry sheets
1¼ sticks butter, melted
1 cup maple syrup, warmed

1 Preheat oven to 425°F. Grease a shallow 11x7-inch baking pan.
2 Coarsely grind the pecans in a food processor, then transfer to a bowl.
Add the sugar and mixed spice, and stir to mix.
3 Unroll the filo pastry and cut in half widthwise to make 2 rectangles.
Place one half on top of the other and cover with plastic wrap to prevent the
filo pastry from drying out.
4 Lay one sheet of filo in the pan, allowing it to extend up the sides. Brush
with melted butter. Layer five more pastry sheets on top, brushing each with
butter and trimming to fit the pan. Sprinkle with one-fifth of the nut mixture.
5 Repeat this process four more times, to give five layers of nut mixture.
Cover with five more sheets of pastry, brushing each with melted butter and
trimming the pastry to fit as you go.
6 Mark the surface of the baklava into 12–20 squares with the tip of a very
sharp knife. Bake for 15 minutes, then lower the setting to 350°F and bake
for another 10–15 minutes until golden.
7 On removing the baklava from the oven, spoon the warm maple syrup over
the surface. Leave to cool in the pan for about 2 hours. Using a sharp knife,
cut into the marked squares to serve.

Crisp, light filo pastry layered with a mildly
spiced pecan nut mixture and drizzled with
maple syrup.

Walnut beignet with coffee cream

Illustrated on previous pages

Serves 6

For the walnut paste
1⅝ cup walnut pieces
scant ¼ cup superfine sugar
1 large egg

For the choux pastry
generous ⅞ cup all-purpose flour
4 tablespoons unsalted butter
⅝ cup water
2 tablespoons superfine sugar
2 large eggs, lightly beaten

For the coffee cream
1 tablespoon espresso coffee powder
generous ⅛ cup light muscovado
  sugar
generous ¼ cup water
1¼ cup heavy cream
2 tablespoons Tia Maria (optional)

To finish
confectioners' sugar, for dusting

1 Preheat oven to 425°F. Grease an 8-inch springform cake pan. Set aside ½ cup walnuts. Process the rest of the nuts in a food processor until finely ground. Add sugar and egg; blend to a soft paste.

2 For the pastry, sift flour onto waxed paper. Heat butter, water, and sugar in a pan until melted, then bring to the boil. Take off the heat, tip in the flour, and beat until the mix leaves the side of the pan. Cool for 2 minutes.

3 Beat in eggs, a little at a time, until smooth and glossy. Spread half the mix in the prepared pan, and dot with the walnut paste. Spread the remaining mix over the top, and scatter with the reserved walnuts, pressing them in gently.

4 Bake for 20 minutes until well risen, then reduce setting to 375°F and bake for another 10 minutes until crisp and golden.

5 Meanwhile, for the coffee cream, gently heat the coffee, sugar, and water in a small pan for 5 minutes. Strain through a fine sieve into a clean pan. Add the cream, and cook for 3 minutes until slightly thickened.

6 Dust the pastry with confectioners' sugar; serve warm, with coffee cream.

A sweet layer of walnut paste makes a delicious filling for crisp, light choux pastry.

Orange syrup tart

Serves 8

For the filling

2 small whole oranges
1 pound 2 ounces corn syrup
¾ cup finely chopped hazelnuts
1¼ cups white breadcrumbs
2 tablespoons lemon juice
2 large eggs, beaten

For the pastry

generous 1½ cups all-purpose flour
1 stick plus 2 tablespoons (10 in all)
   unsalted butter, diced
1 egg yolk
1 tablespoon caster sugar
2 tablespoons cold water

1 Put the oranges in a small pan, just cover with boiling water, and simmer gently for 30 minutes or until the skins are soft. Drain; leave to cool.

2 To make the pastry, blend the flour and butter in a food processor until the mixture resembles breadcrumbs. Add the egg yolk, sugar, and water. Mix briefly to a smooth dough. Wrap and chill for 30 minutes.

3 Preheat oven to 400°F. Roll out the pastry on a lightly floured surface and use to line a 10-inch false-bottomed cake pan. Line with waxed paper and baking beans, and bake blind for 15 minutes. Remove paper and beans; bake for another 5 minutes.

4 Halve the cooked oranges, discard any seeds, and blend to a purée. Warm the corn syrup in a pan until slightly thinned. Stir in the nuts, breadcrumbs, orange purée, and lemon juice, then the eggs.

5 Turn into the pastry shell, and bake for about 30 minutes until the filling is pale golden but not firmly set. Let cool slightly before serving.

Puréed oranges give this tempting deep syrup tart a wonderful tangy flavor.

Coconut and mango meringue pie

Illustrated on previous pages

Serves 8
1¼ cups all-purpose flour
6 tablespoons unsalted butter
3 large egg yolks
scant ⅛ cup superfine sugar
For the filling and topping
2 medium, ripe mangoes, peeled

2 tablespoons cornstarch
⅝ cup orange juice
⅞ cup sugar
3 large eggs, separated
¾ cup finely grated coconut
toasted coconut shavings (optional)

1 Make pastry as for Amaretti and apricot tart (page 278). Wrap and chill for 30 minutes.
2 Preheat oven to 400°F. Roll out the pastry thinly on a lightly floured surface and use to line an 8-inch loose-bottomed quiche pan, about 1½ inches deep. Bake blind for 20 minutes, then remove paper and baking beans and bake for another 5 minutes. Increase setting to 425°F.
3 Slice 1 mango, discarding stone; arrange in the pastry shell. Purée the flesh from the other mango in a blender until smooth.
4 In a pan, mix the cornstarch with 2 tablespoons orange juice. Add remaining orange juice, mango purée, and ⅛ cup sugar. Bring to the boil, stirring until thickened. Beat in the egg yolks. Turn into the pastry shell.
5 For the meringue, whisk egg whites in a clean bowl until stiff. Gradually whisk in the remaining sugar, a spoonful at a time, until the meringue is stiff and glossy. Fold in the grated coconut, then spoon the filling over. Bake for 5–10 minutes until the meringue is golden. Cool before serving, topped with coconut shavings, if liked.

An exotic version of lemon meringue pie.

Mocha fudge torte

Serves 6–8

5 ounces dark chocolate, in pieces
6 tablespoons butter, cut into cubes
¾ cup ground almonds
3 medium eggs, separated
⅝ cup superfine sugar
1 tablespoon coffee powder

For the syrup

24 coffee beans
¾ cup superfine sugar
½ cup water
4 tablespoons kahlúa or other coffee
  liqueur

1 Preheat oven to 350°F. Line the base of an 8-inch springform cake pan with waxed paper. Melt the chocolate in a heatproof bowl over a pan of simmering water. Add the butter and leave until melted. Remove from the heat and stir in the ground almonds.

2 Whisk egg yolks, sugar, and coffee powder together in a large bowl, using an electric blender, until thickened. Add the chocolate mixture and fold in.

3 Whisk the egg whites in a clean bowl until stiff, then gently fold into the mixture. Pour into the prepared cake pan, and bake for 30–40 minutes until crusty on top; it should still be slightly soft in the middle. Leave to cool in the pan, then remove.

4 For the syrup, put the coffee beans, sugar, and water in a heavy-based pan over a low heat until the sugar is dissolved, then increase the heat and boil for 5 minutes until syrupy. Add the liqueur and pour into a bowl; cool. Cover and chill until required.

5 Serve the torte, cut into wedges and drizzled with the coffee syrup.

Note Make the torte a day ahead for convenince, and keep chilled until ready to serve.

An irresistible dessert enhanced with a rich coffee syrup—best served with light cream.

Chocolate star anise cake with coffee syrup

12 slices

8 ounces good-quality dark chocolate

1 stick unsalted butter

4 large eggs, plus 2 egg yolks

½ cup superfine sugar

scant ⅜ cup all-purpose flour, sifted

2 teaspoons ground star anise

scant 1 cup fresh white breadcrumbs

For the syrup

1¼ cup strong black coffee

½ cup sugar

2 tablespoons Kahlúa or other coffee liqueur

1 star anise

1 Preheat oven to 375°F. Grease and base line a deep 8-inch round cake pan. Melt the chocolate and butter together in a bowl set over a pan of gently simmering water. Let cool slightly.

2 Put the eggs, egg yolks, and sugar in a bowl; whisk until pale and thickened. Sift the flour, then sift again, with the star anise, over the mixture. Add breadcrumbs and melted chocolate; fold in carefully using a large metal spoon.

3 Spoon the mixture into the prepared pan and level the surface. Bake for 35 minutes or until a skewer inserted into the center comes out clean.

4 Meanwhile, make the syrup. Put the coffee and sugar in a heavy-based pan, and heat gently until the sugar is dissolved. Increase heat and boil for 5 minutes until reduced and thickened slightly. Stir in the coffee liqueur and star anise; keep warm.

5 Pierce the surface of the cake with a skewer, then drizzle half of the coffee syrup over. Set aside to cool. Serve cut into wedges, with the remaining coffee syrup and crème fraîche.

Variation Replace star anise with the crushed seeds from 3 cardamom pods.

Note Ground star anise is available from some supermarkets and Asian grocery stores. Alternatively, buy whole star anise and grind them yourself, using a spice grinder or pestle and mortar.

A superb chocolate cake, flavored with star anise and soaked in a coffee syrup as it cools.

Pear, pine nut, and lemon strudel

Illustrated on previous pages

Serves 4
2 ripe pears
finely grated rind of 1 lemon
2 tablespoons lemon juice
4 tablespoons unsalted butter
scant 1 cup pine nuts

scant 1 cup white breadcrumbs
⅛ cup light muscovado sugar
generous 3 tablespoons clear honey,
  such as orange blossom
¼ pound filo pastry
confectioners' sugar, for dusting

1 Preheat oven to 400°F. Peel, core and thinly slice the pears crosswise. Immerse in a bowl of cold water with 1 tablespoon of the lemon juice added.
2 Melt 1 tablespoon butter in a skillet and fry the pine nuts until pale golden. Add the breadcrumbs and fry gently until golden.
3 Drain the pears, dry on paper towels, and put in a bowl with the breadcrumb and pine nut mixture, sugar, and lemon rind.
4 Melt another 1 tablespoon butter. Keep one sheet of filo pastry for the topping, well wrapped to prevent it from drying out. Layer the remaining sheets on a clean surface, brushing each with a little melted butter.
5 Spoon the filling on top to within 1 inch of the edges. Drizzle with the honey and lemon juice; dot with remaining firm butter. Fold the short ends over the filling, then roll up, starting at a long side. Lift onto a lightly greased baking sheet, join uppermost.
6 Brush with any remaining melted butter, then crumple the reserved filo sheet around the strudel. Bake for about 25 minutes until golden. Cool slightly, then dust with confectioners' sugar. Serve warm, cut into slices, with Greek yogurt or crème fraîche.

Upside down cider apple cake

Serves 8

2 Granny Smith apples
2 tablespoons unsalted butter
scant ¼ cup granulated sugar
1 stick butter, softened
⅝ cup light muscovado sugar

grated rind of 1 lemon
2 large eggs, beaten
3 tablespoons dry hard cider
1¼ cups self-rising flour
1 teaspoon ground mixed spice
generous ¼ cup golden raisins

1 Preheat oven to 350°F. Grease the side of a deep 8-inch round cake pan (but not springform).

2 Peel, core, and thickly slice the apples. Heat the unsalted butter and granulated sugar in a large, heavy-based skillet until the butter is melted and the sugar starts to brown. Add the apple slices, and fry for 1–2 minutes each side until golden. Cool slightly.

3 Cream the softened butter, muscovado sugar, and lemon rind together in a bowl until fluffy, then beat in the eggs, cider, flour, and spice until smooth. Fold in the raisins.

4 Arrange the apples over the base of the cake pan, adding any pan juices. Spoon the cake mixture on top and spread evenly. Bake for 30–35 minutes until a skewer inserted in the middle comes out clean.

5 Leave in the pan for 10 minutes, then invert onto a wire rack and leave to cool. Serve warm.

This is excellent served warm for dessert, with ice cream or whipped cream.

Saffron rum babas

Serves 6

2 tablespoons milk

pinch saffron strands

2 cups all-purpose flour, sifted

pinch of salt

2 tablespoons superfine sugar

1 teaspoon fast action dried yeast

2 large eggs, lightly beaten

4 tablespoons butter, melted

For the syrup

3½ ounces sugar

6 tablespoons rum

1 teaspoon pomegranate syrup

To serve

lightly whipped cream

1 pomegranate, seeds extracted

1 Grease 6 small timbales or baba molds. Heat the milk with the saffron almost to the boil, then set aside to infuse until tepid.

2 Mix the flour, salt, sugar, and yeast in a bowl. Make a well in the center, and add the milk, eggs, and butter. Mix to a soft, sticky dough, then beat thoroughly for 5 minutes.

3 Spoon into the molds, cover loosely with oiled plastic wrap, and leave in a warm place for 1 hour or until the dough is risen almost to the tops of the molds; remove plastic wrap.

4 Preheat oven to 400°F. Bake for 15 minutes until risen and golden.

5 For the syrup, dissolve the sugar in 1 cup water in a pan over a low heat, then boil for 3 minutes until syrupy. Cool, then stir in the rum and pomegranate syrup.

6 Unmold babas, cool slightly, then stand in a shallow dish. Pour on two-thirds of the syrup and leave to soak for 30 minutes.

7 Serve the babas drizzled with syrup and topped with cream and pomegranate seeds.

Divine saffron babas, flavored with a pomegranate and rum syrup.

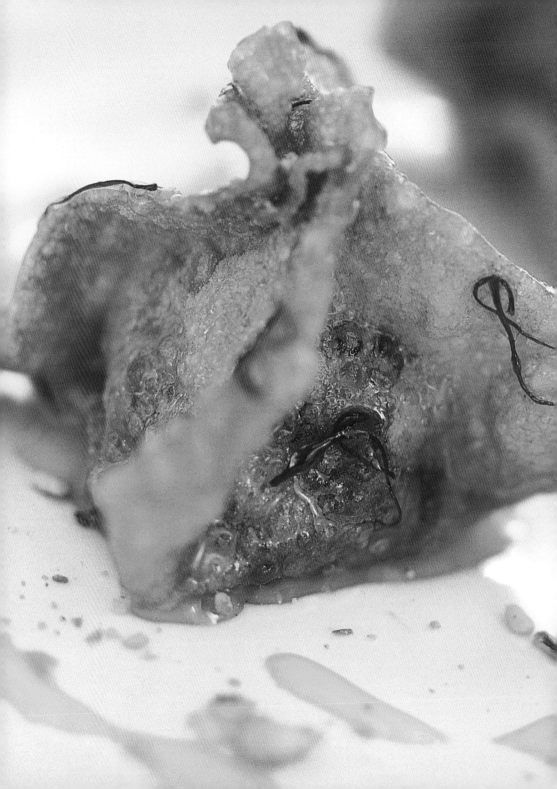

Date and pistachio wontons

Illustrated on previous pages

large pinch of saffron strands
generous 1 cup superfine sugar
½ cup water
generous 1 cup shelled pistachio nuts

12 medjool dates, stoned and chopped
4 tablespoons rosewater essence
12 wonton wrappers
vegetable oil for deep-frying

1 Put the saffron, sugar, and water in a heavy-based pan over a low heat to dissolve the sugar. Increase heat and boil for 3 minutes until syrupy.
2 Put the pistachio nuts in a food processor and process until roughly ground. Remove about one-third and reserve for dusting.
3 Add the dates, 2 tablespoons rosewater, and 3 tablespoons syrup to the processor, and mix to a paste. Add the remaining rosewater to the syrup.
4 Put a spoonful of paste in the center of each wonton wrapper, brush the edges with water, and draw up over the filling; press together to seal. Cover with plastic wrap until ready to cook.
5 Heat the oil in a deep saucepan to a depth of 3–4 inches and a temperature of 325°F, measured with a thermometer. Fry the wontons in batches for 30 seconds until golden; drain on paper towels. Shortly before serving, reheat the syrup. Bathe the wontons in the hot syrup just before serving.
6 To serve, put 3 wontons on each plate, drizzle with some of the hot syrup, and dust with the reserved crushed pistachios. Serve with crème fraîche.

Fried wontons filled with a scented paste, bathed in a saffron and rosewater syrup, then dusted with crushed pistachios.

Wild berry roulade with pastis

Serves 6

For the sponge

3 large eggs

⅜ cup superfine sugar

½ cup all-purpose flour

⅛ cup cornstarch

2 teaspoons orange flower water

For the filling

1 pound 2 ounces mixed berries, such as raspberries, sliced strawberries, blackberries, and blueberries

3 tablespoons pastis, such as Ricard or Pernod

1 tablespoon clear honey

2 tablespoons low-fat crème fraîche

2 tablespoons yogurt

1 Preheat oven to 425°F. Grease and line a 13x9inch jelly roll pan. Put the fruit in a bowl, add the pastis and honey, and toss gently to mix. Set aside to macerate for about 1 hour.

2 To make the cake, whisk eggs and sugar in a bowl, using an electric beater, for about 5 minutes, until the mixture is foamy, and double in volume.

3 Sift flour and cornstarch over the mix, and fold in the orange flower water.

4 Turn the mixture into the prepared pan and spread gently and evenly with a spatula. Bake for 8–10 minutes until well risen and just springy to the touch; do not overcook.

5 Invert the cake onto a wire rack, peel off lining paper, then trim the edges. Lay a clean dish towel on top, and carefully roll up the warm cake with the cloth inside; leave to cool.

6 For the filling, combine the crème fraîche and yogurt in a bowl. Drain the macerated fruit, reserving the juice, then fold into the yogurt mixture.

7 Carefully unroll cake and remove dish towel. Spoon two-thirds of the filling evenly over the surface, and carefully roll up again. Place on a serving dish, with the join underneath. Chill for 1–2 hours before serving.

8 Mix the remaining fruit with the reserved juice to make a sauce. Serve the roulade, cut into slices, with the berry sauce.

A light, airy fatless sponge rolled around flavored summer berries.

Amaretti and apricot tart

Illustrated on previous pages

Serves 8

For the pastry

1¼ cups plain flour

6 tablespoons unsalted butter

3 large egg yolks

scant ¼ cup superfine sugar

For the filling

1¼ cups dried apricots, sliced

3 tablespoons Grand Marnier

28 amaretti cookies, halved

2 large eggs, plus 1 egg yolk

generous ⅛ cup superfine sugar

4 tablespoons unsalted butter, melted

1¼ cups heavy cream

1¼ cups milk

For the syrup

pinch saffron strands, soaked in
  1 tablespoon boiling water

⅜ cup superfine sugar

1 cup water

To finish

confectioners' sugar, for dusting

1 To make the pastry, put the flour and butter in a food processor and process until the mixture resembles fine breadcrumbs. Add the egg yolks and sugar and mix briefly to a firm dough. Wrap and chill for 30 minutes.

2 Preheat oven to 400°F. Roll out the pastry on a floured surface and use to line a 9½-inch flan tin, 1½-inch deep. Line with waxed paper and baking beans, and bake blind for 15 minutes. Remove paper and beans; bake for 5 minutes. Reduce to 325°F.

3 Soak apricots in liqueur for 15 minutes. Scatter cookies in the pastry shell.

4 Beat eggs, yolk, sugar, and butter together in a bowl. Bring cream and milk to the boil, then whisk into the egg mix. Strain custard into the pastry shell, scatter half of the apricots over, and bake for 25–30 minutes until set.

5 For the syrup, dissolve sugar in the water in a pan on a low heat, then boil for 5 minutes until syrupy. Stir in the saffron, remaining apricots, and liqueur. Dust the tart with confectioners' sugar, and serve with the saffron syrup.

Crushed cookies and apricots, set in a creamy custard within a rich pastry shell. A saffron and almond syrup is the perfect complement.

Plum and almond butter puffs

Makes 6

4 tablespoons unsalted butter, softened

scant ⅛ cup superfine sugar

½ cup ground almonds

½ teaspoon almond extract

¾ pound ready-made puff pastry

1 pound 8 ounces red plums, halved and stoned

beaten egg, to glaze

1 tablespoon slivered or flaked almonds

2 tablespoons confectioners' sugar

1 Beat 2 tablespoons butter with the sugar, ground almonds, and almond extract to a stiff paste.

2 Roll out half the pastry on a lightly floured surface, and cut out six 4-inch circles; lay on a lightly greased baking sheet. Spread to ½ inch from the edges with the almond paste. Roll out the remaining pastry and cut out circles, as above. Position over the filling. With the tip of a sharp knife, cut a shallow rim, ½ inch from the edge of each round. Chill for 30 minutes.

3 Preheat oven to 410°F. Cut the plums into thick wedges and scatter over the pastry rounds, within the cut rim.

4 Brush the pastry edges with egg, then scatter with the almonds. Bake for 10 minutes until risen and golden. Dot with the remaining butter, dust with confectioners' sugar and bake for another 10–12 minutes until deep golden. Serve with whipped cream, if desired.

Ready-made puff pastry disks sandwiched with almond paste, and baked with a fresh plum topping for a quick and easy dessert.

Passion fruit brûlées

4 large egg yolks
¼ teaspoon vanilla extract
1 tablespoon cornstarch
2 tablespoons superfine sugar
scant 1¼ cups cream
2 passion fruit, halved
For the caramel topping
8 tablespoons superfine sugar

1 Whisk the egg yolks, vanilla extract, cornstarch and sugar together
in a bowl until evenly blended.
2 Heat the cream in a heavy-based pan to just below the boil. Pour onto the
egg yolk mixture, whisking all the time. Return to the pan, and cook,
whisking constantly, until the custard thickens; do not boil. If the custard
starts to become lumpy, quickly take off the heat and whisk briskly until
smooth, then continue.
3 Scoop seeds and pulp from the passion fruit into a sieve over a bowl; rub
to separate the juice from the seeds. Stir the passion fruit juice into the custard
with ½ teaspoon of the seeds. Pour into 4 small ramekins or other ovenproof
dishes. Chill for 2–3 hours until set, or up to 24 hours if preparing ahead.
4 To make the caramel topping, sprinkle sugar evenly over each custard
and put under a preheated hot broiler until the sugar melts and caramelizes.
5 Chill for 2–3 hours until the caramel is set hard before serving.

Note If you have a blowtorch, use this to caramelize the topping.

Passion fruit adds a refreshing contrast to the
irresistible creaminess of classic crème brûlée.

Caramelized rice tartlets

Illustrated on previous pages

Makes 8
For the pastry
generous 1¼ cup all-purpose flour
1¼ sticks (10 tablespoons) unsalted
   butter
4–5 teaspoons cold water

For the filling
scant ⅜ cup flaked rice
2 cups milk
1 vanilla bean
generous ⅜ cup sugar
⅝ cup heavy cream
2 large eggs, beaten

1 To make the pastry, blend the flour and butter in a food processor until the mixture resembles fine breadcrumbs. Add the water, and process briefly to a firm dough. Chill for 30 minutes.

2 Preheat oven to 400°F. Roll out the pastry thinly on a lightly floured surface and use to line eight 3½-inch individual false-bottomed quiche pans. Line the pastry shells with waxed paper and baking beans and bake blind for 15 minutes. Remove the paper and beans; bake for a further 5 minutes. Reduce oven setting to 350°F.

3 Put the rice, milk, vanilla bean, and a generous ⅛ cup sugar in a heavy-based pan. Bring to the boil, reduce the heat, and simmer gently for about 8 minutes until the rice is tender and the mixture is thickened. Leave to cool slightly. Remove the vanilla bean, then beat in the cream and eggs.

4 Pour the filling into the tartlet shells, and bake for 5–8 minutes until very lightly set. Preheat broiler to moderate. Sprinkle the remaining sugar in an even layer over the tartlets, and broil for about 4 minutes until lightly caramelized. Serve warm or cold, with sugared raspberries or strawberries.

Tartlet cases with a light, creamy rice filling, baked until softly set, then topped with sugar, and caramelized. Best served with berry fruits.

Meringue roulade with melba fruits

Serves 8

For the meringue

3 large egg whites

¾ cup superfine sugar

1 tablespoon cornstarch

2 teaspoons vanilla extract

1 teaspoon white wine vinegar

For the melba filling

scant 1¼ cups heavy cream

2 tablespoons confectioners' sugar, plus extra for rolling

2 tablespoons peach schnapps or dessert wine

1 large peach, peeled, stoned, and diced

1 cup raspberries

1 Preheat oven to 275°F. Line an 11x9-inch jelly roll pan with baking parchment.

2 Whisk the egg whites in a clean bowl until stiff, then gradually whisk in the sugar, a tablespoonful at a time, until stiff and glossy.

3 Quickly and carefully fold in the cornstarch, vanilla, and vinegar. Spoon into the prepared tin and spread very gently to the edges.

4 Bake for 35 minutes until set. On removing from the oven, cover the meringue with a slightly damp dish towel and leave to cool.

5 To serve, lightly whip the cream with the sugar and schnapps or wine. Dust a sheet of nonstick baking parchment with confectioners' sugar. Turn the meringue onto the paper, then spread with the cream and scatter the fruit over. Roll up carefully and place on a plate. If preparing ahead, refrigerate for up to 4 hours until required. Dust with confectioners' sugar to serve.

A luscious mallowy meringue rolled around a peach and raspberry filling.

Trio of mango

Serves 4–6

1¼ cup sugar
juice of 3 lemons
4 large or 6 medium ripe mangoes
1¼ cups heavy cream
15-ounce can lychees in syrup

1 Put the sugar, lemon juice, and 4 tablespoons water in a heavy-based pan over a low heat until the sugar is dissolved. Increase the heat and boil until syrupy. Allow to cool.

2 Peel the mangoes, cut the flesh from the stones, and put in a blender with the sugar syrup. Blend to a purée. Transfer 6 tablespoons purée to a bowl and reserve for the sauce.

3 Transfer two-thirds of the remaining mango purée to an ice cream maker (if you have one); mix in the cream, and churn according to the manufacturer's instructions. Or pour the purée and cream into a freezerproof container, stir well, and freeze for 1½ hours until partially frozen, then turn into a food processor and mix until smooth. Refreeze, repeat once more, then freeze until required.

4 For the sorbet, drain lychees over a bowl to catch the syrup. Add the lychees with ⅝ cup of their syrup to the mango purée in the blender, and purée. Freeze following instructions for freezing ice cream.

5 Add the remaining lychee syrup to the mango purée reserved for the sauce. Mix well, cover, and chill.

6 If necessary, soften the ice cream and sorbet in the fridge for 20 minutes before serving. Serve the sorbet in a separate little dish set on a large plate with a scoop of ice cream and a swirl of mango sauce. Scatter with rose petals to decorate, if wished.

This is a perfect finale to a special dinner. Matching fresh rose petals lend a fragrant finishing touch.

Rosewater pashka

Illustrated on previous pages

Serves 6

1 pound 2 ounces ricotta cheese

2 large egg yolks

6 tablespoons crème fraîche

2 teaspoons rosewater essence

4 tablespoons butter, softened

scant ¼ cup superfine sugar

⅜ cup chopped candied fruits, such as pineapple, cherries and citrus peel

scant ¼ cup raisins

⅛ cup chopped pistachio nuts

To serve

few chopped pistachio nuts

orange slices (optional)

1 Line a 4-cup capacity mixing bowl with muslin, allowing plenty to overhang the rim. Tip the cheese into a sieve to drain off any whey, then turn into a bowl. Beat in the egg yolks, crème fraîche, and rosewater.

2 Cream the butter and sugar together in another bowl, then add to the cheese mixture and beat thoroughly until smooth. Stir in the fruits, raisins, and pistachios.

3 Spoon the mixture into the lined bowl. Cover the surface with the overhanging muslin, then invert the basin and place muslin side down on a wire rack over a tray.

4 Refrigerate overnight, or for up to 3 days if preparing ahead. As the mixture chills it becomes firmer.

5 To serve, remove the bowl and muslin. Spoon the pashka onto serving plates, and scatter with pistachios. Serve with orange slices, if liked, and cookies.

Rosewater adds a floral note to this delectable Russian dessert.

Rum punch trifle with exotic fruits

Serves 6–8

small pound cake (approx. ½ pound)
1 small pineapple, peeled, cored, and
   chopped
1 mango, peeled, stoned, and chopped
2 bananas, peeled and thickly sliced
juice and grated rind of 1 lime

juice of 1 orange
3 tablespoons confectioners' sugar
⅜ cup dark rum
3½ cups canned custard (see note)
1¼ cups heavy cream, lightly
   whipped
mint sprigs, to decorate

1 Slice the pound cake and use to cover the base of a large glass serving bowl. Toss the fruits with the lime juice and orange juice, confectioners' sugar, and rum, then scatter over the cake.

2 Pour the custard evenly over the fruit. Cover with the whipped cream, and chill for 2–3 hours, or up to 2 days if desired.

3 Serve topped with the lime rind and mint.

Note Canned custard from Britain is available in the gourmet food section of many supermarkets. An alternative is Bird's custard powder. To use this in the recipe, mix 3 tablespoons with ¼ cup milk in a bowl until smooth. Heat another 3½ cups milk in a heavy-based pan until boiling; whisk into the custard mix. Pour back into the pan, add 4 tablespoons superfine sugar, and stir over the heat until thickened. Cook, stirring, for 1 minute. Allow to cool slightly.

Tropical fruits and plenty of rum give this trifle a Caribbean twist.

Poached tamarillos with pink panna cotta

Illustrated on previous pages

9 ounces superfine sugar
4 star anise
½ cup grenadine
⅝ cup water
4 tamarillos, stalks intact

scant 2 cups heavy cream
2 teaspoons vanilla extract
2 ounces white chocolate
1 teaspoon powdered gelatine

1 Put the sugar, star anise, grenadine, and water in a heavy-based pan over a low heat until the sugar is dissolved. Increase the heat and bring to a simmer.

2 Cut a cross in the skin at the pointed end of each tamarillo. Add to the sugar syrup, cover, and poach gently, turning occasionally, for 10–15 minutes until just soft; test with a skewer. Leave in the syrup for 24 hours.

3 Meanwhile, make the panna cotta. Slowly heat the cream in a heavy-based pan over a very low heat until bubbles start to appear around the edge; this should take 10–15 minutes. Take off the heat, and add the vanilla and chocolate; stir until melted.

4 Measure ⅝ cup of the poaching syrup into a small heatproof dish. Sprinkle over the gelatine, leave to soften for a few minutes, then stand over a pan of simmering water until dissolved. Stir into the cream.

5 Pour into four ⅝-cup oval darioles or other molds and chill for 24 hours until set.

6 To unmold the panna cotta, dip the molds briefly into hot water, then invert onto plates. Place a tamarillo on each plate and spoon some of the syrup over to serve.

Teamed with panna cotta, tamarillos make a stylish prepare-ahead dessert.

Sicilian cassata

Serves 10–12

¾ pound bought all-butter pound cake

⅝ cup cassis or framboise liqueur

1 pound 10 ounces ricotta cheese

1¼ cup confectioners' sugar, sifted

⅝ cup heavy cream

1⅜ cup mixed ready-to-eat exotic dried fruits (papaya, pineapple, mango and melon), finely diced

scant ½ cup glazed cherries, minced

¼ pound dark, bitter chocolate, chopped

½ cup shelled pistachio nuts, chopped

3 tablespoons Strega liqueur or marsala

glazed or fresh cherries on stalks to decorate (optional)

1 Cut the cake into ½-inch thick, long slices, and brush one side with cassis. Use to line the side and base of a 9-inch springform cake pan, placing the brushed sides outwards and trimming to fit the pan as necessary, so there are no gaps. Brush the inside of the case with cassis, then chill.

2 In a large bowl, whisk the ricotta with the sugar together until smooth. Whip the cream in another bowl until it forms soft peaks, then fold into the ricotta mixture.

3 Fold in the dried fruits, cherries, chocolate and pistachios, then the liqueur. Spoon the mixture into the prepared pan, and freeze for at least 10 hours until firm and easy to slice.

4 Unmold the cassata onto a plate. Cut into wedges, and serve each portion topped with a cherry on a stalk, if wished.

Note If the cassata has been frozen for longer than 10 hours, transfer to the fridge 30 minutes before serving to soften slightly.

An elegant frozen ricotta cake, richly flavoured with exotic dried fruit, cherries, dark chocolate, and pistachios.

Florentine baskets

Makes 10
4 tablespoons unsalted butter
scant ¼ cup superfine sugar
generous ⅛ cup corn syrup
⅜ cup all-purpose flour
⅛ cup mixed crystallized or glazed
fruit, such as pineapple, ginger,
cherries, and/or angelica
¼ cup blanched almonds or shelled
pistachio nuts, chopped
¼ teaspoon grated lemon rind
5 ounces dark chocolate, melted

1 Preheat oven to 350°F.
2 Melt the butter, sugar, and corn syrup together in a pan over a low heat.
Off the heat, stir in the flour, fruit, nuts, and lemon rind; mix well.
3 Drop 3 or 4 teaspoonfuls of the mixture onto nonstick or greased baking
sheets, spacing well apart to allow for spreading. Bake for 10 minutes until
golden brown.
4 Allow the cookies to cool very slightly until starting to firm up, then
quickly lift each one with a spatula and drape over an upturned dariole mold
or small tumbler. Using your fingers, carefully press into a basket shape,
fluting the edges.
5 Repeat with the remaining mixture; leave baskets until cool and set firm.
6 Melt the chocolate in a heatproof bowl over a pan of simmering water.
Carefully release each basket from its mold, and dip the base into the
chocolate to coat. Place the baskets, chocolate side up, on a wire rack, and
leave until set.
7 Just before serving, fill the baskets with scoops of ice cream.

Variation Use good-quality white chocolate instead of dark. Dip the rims
of the baskets rather than the bases into the melted white chocolate to give
an attractive edging.

These crisp fruit and nut baskets make pretty
containers for ice cream.

Iced pear parfait

Serves 6

1 cup superfine sugar

1 cup water

6 ripe flavorful pears

4 tablespoons Poire William liqueur

1¼ cup heavy cream

1 small egg white

1 Put the sugar and water in a heavy-based pan and dissolve over a low heat, then increase the heat and boil until syrupy.

2 Using a mandolin or very sharp knife, cut 6–12 very thin slices lengthwise from the central part of 2 pears, keeping the peel, core, and stalk intact. Lay them in the syrup.

3 Peel and core the rest of these 2 pears, and the other 4 pears. Roughly chop the flesh, and put into a heavy-based pan with the Poire William. Cover and cook over a low heat for about 8 minutes until soft, checking to make sure they don't stick. Transfer the pears and liqueur to a blender and purée. Turn into a large bowl and cool.

4 Preheat oven to 230°F. Carefully drain the pear slices and lay on a silicone-lined baking tray, reserving excess syrup. Put in the oven for 2 hours until crisp, but not colored. Peel off the paper. Store in an airtight container between paper towels for up to 2 days.

5 Whip half the cream in a bowl to soft peaks, then fold into the cooled pear purée. In a clean bowl, whisk the egg white until stiff, then add 3 tablespoons of the reserved syrup and whisk until glossy. Gently fold into the pear purée.

6 Spoon the parfait mixture into six 4–5-ounce timbales or dariole moulds, level the tops and freeze for at least 8 hours.

7 To make the butterscotch sauce, boil the remaining sugar syrup to a golden caramel color. Take off the heat, and then pour in the rest of the cream, taking care, as it will splutter; stir well to dissolve the caramel.

8 To unmold the parfaits, stand molds in cold water for 30 seconds, invert onto a cake server and transfer to a tray. Store in freezer until ready to serve.

9 To serve, warm the butterscotch sauce. Place a parfait on each serving plate, and drizzle with butterscotch sauce. Decorate with the pear chips.

Delicate parfaits, wafer-thin pear chips, and butterscotch sauce can all be made in advance.

Index

Acknowledgments

The publishers wish to thank the following for the loan of props for photography:
The Conran Shop, Michelin House, 81 Fulham Road, London SW3 (0207 589 7401); **Divertimenti**, 139–141 Fulham Road, London SW3 (0207 581 8065); **Divertimenti**, 45–7 Wigmore Street, London W1 (0207 935 0689); **Designers Guild**, 277 Kings Road, London SW3 (0207 351 5775); **Habitat**, 196 Tottenham Court Road, London W1 (0207 631 3880); **Ikea**, Purley Way, Croydon (0208 208 5607); **Inventory**, 26–40 Kensington High Street, London W8 (0207 937 2626); **Jerry's**, 163–7 Fulham Road, London SW3 (0207 581 0909); **LSA International**, The Dolphin Estate, Windmill Road, Sunbury on Thames, Middlesex (01932 789 721); **Muji**, 26 Great Marlborough Street, London W1 (0207 494 1197)

Food Stylists Maxine Clark, Joanna Farrow, Marie Ange Lapierre, Louise Pickford, Bridget Sargeson, Linda Tubby
Photographic Stylists Kasha Harmer Hirst, Maya Babic
Contributors Sara Buenfeld, Maxine Clark, Joanna Farrow, Janet Illsley, Louise Pickford, Bridget Sargeson, Linda Tubby, Sunil Vijayakar